# LATIN AMERICA

# LATIN AMERICA

## The beauty, the magic – take a journey of a lifetime!

# PaRragon

Bath · New York · Singapore · Hong Kong · Cologne · Delhi · Melbourne

First published by Parragon in 2009

Parragon
Queen Street House
4 Queen Street
Bath BA1 1HE, UK

Designed, produced, and packaged by
Stonecastle Graphics Limited

Text by Gill Davies
Designed by Paul Turner and Sue Pressley
Edited by Philip de Ste. Croix
Picture research by Harry Sharp and Karen James

ISBN 978-1-4075-4738-1

Printed in China

**Page 1:** *A young woman from Peru in a gloriously colored costume holds a tiny lamb. The Spaniards introduced sheep to the Americas and, although they were not so hardy as cattle, their numbers grew steadily in some areas, providing useful mutton, sheepskin, and wool.*

**Pages 2–3:** *Snowy mountains in Chile, where the contrasting scenery includes towering Andean peaks, volcanoes, ancient forests, and many superb lakes.*

**Background:** *Mist rises above the gleaming surface of Bolivia's Salar de Uyuni, the world's largest salt flat and the breeding ground for three Latin American flamingo species—Chilean, James's, and Andean.*

# Contents

# Introduction

When Christopher Columbus set sail in 1492 across uncharted seas in search of a westward passage to the Orient he discovered not only the Bahamas, Cuba, and Hispaniola but found that, beyond these gorgeous islands, an unexpected giant continent lay waiting—the amazing New World which he would soon visit on his subsequent voyages of exploration. In his wake many Spanish and Portuguese explorers and emigrants arrived to settle here—and to impose their culture, lifestyles, and religion on the indigenous peoples. Because the language of these conquistadores was based on Latin, the region became known as Latin America.

South of Mexico, the narrow twist of land linking North and South America includes Belize, Costa Rica, El Salvador, Guatemala, Honduras, Nicaragua, and the final narrow sliver of Panama—with the Caribbean islands and Cuba glinting in the sea to the east of this. Beyond Panama the giant continent of South America swells like a busy bees' nest, humming with the bustle of many nations, with Brazil occupying the largest portion—over half the land and people in South America are Brazilian. The other nations are Argentina, Bolivia, Chile, Colombia, Ecuador, French Guiana, Guyana, Paraguay, Peru, Suriname, Uruguay, and Venezuela.

*Above:* The Peruvian pututo is a musical instrument made from a shell.

*Left:* Costa Rica's superbly rich rainforest habitat supports an amazing variety of mammals, birds, reptiles, amphibians, fish, and insects.

The Pacific and Atlantic Oceans wash west and east coasts respectively. The Pacific was called the 'peaceful sea' by Portuguese explorer Ferdinand Magellan but this name seems singularly inappropriate at the wild southern tip of Cape Horn, where huge crashing seas pummel vessels daring to navigate through this place of elemental energy. Wind, sea, rock, ice, and rain converge at the continent's southern tip and the combination has claimed the lives of many unfortunate sailors. Having encompassed hot deserts and dripping rainforests during its sweep south, Latin America finally points toward the cold Antarctic.

This book explores the multifaceted Latin American world from two main viewpoints: first it considers the places—contrasting dramatic landscapes from mountain peaks and fiery volcanoes to seascapes and idyllic islands, voyaging along mighty rivers and through dense jungles, past thundering waterfalls, through grassy plains and pampas, swamps and wetlands, desolate saltpans, and dazzling deserts. It pauses to observe the amazing wildlife in Amazonian rainforests, where brilliant butterflies flit through sunlit clearings, snakes slide effortlessly through the jungle understory and pale streaked orchids dot the leafy floor. In the rocky Galápagos Islands special creatures like giant tortoises, marine iguanas, lively finches, and blue-footed booby birds were, in 1835, the inspiration that led Charles Darwin to elucidate his theory of evolution. Throughout Latin America, the kaleidoscope of natural wildlife contributes to a myriad images with every different creature—whether in water, on land, or soaring in the skies above—contributing a vital element to this amazing tapestry of landscapes.

## People, History, and Life Today

The second part of the book discovers the people of Latin America—tracing their colorful history and marveling at the awe-inspiring pyramids, temples, and palaces that are the visible reminders of exciting civilizations like the Mayans, Aztecs, and Incas. Many intrepid explorers from Europe traveled here to find yet more wild territory while pirates patrolled the waves eager to seize the hoards of silver and gold which had been loaded into treasure galleons for transportation back to the Old World. Today tourists flock to see some of the world's most spectacular archaeological sites—the Mayan city of Chichén Itzá on the Yucatán peninsula; stunning Machu Picchu in the mountains of Peru, sometimes hiding its Inca secrets as its lofty settlements disappear into the swirling clouds; the stern enigmatic statues on Easter Island, standing sentinel to a mysterious past.

The way of life today—urban and rural—is revealed from scintillating Havana and Mexico City to vibrant Buenos Aires, ancient Cuzco, and exotic Rio de Janeiro where carnivals and fireworks dazzle crowds of spectators.

These busy nations have successful industries, growing populations, and expanding cities, so dealing with the increasing threat posed by deforestation demands sensitive but firm regulations. As the impact of climate change escalates, the Latin American nations are, indeed, making concerted efforts to establish effective conservation movements and to support growing numbers of nature reserves, to provide wildlife with a refuge from human expansion, and to limit the worst impacts of destructive logging and the encroachment of agriculture which threaten unique habitats. The vast forest cover of Amazonia plays a major role in maintaining the stability of the entire world's climate, so this is not merely a national or continental issue—it is of global importance.

Latin America is home to a wealth of wildlife to preserve for future generations. Our tour spotlights numerous fascinating species—from aptly-named spectacled bears to playful monkeys, from sloths edging slowly beneath tree branches to giant anteaters and armadillos searching for food in the undergrowth below. Llamas and alpacas graze the high mountain pastures, alert for predatory cougars, while rattlesnakes and scorpions seek cool shade in the deserts by day, emerging at dusk to hunt. Anacondas glide along rivers, their noses breaking through silvery-bubbled water—a habitat they share with razor-toothed piranhas and sleepy-looking caimans. Venomous fer-de-lance snakes lie in wait for their prey and brightly colored poison-arrow frogs cling to waterside plants. In the azure skies condors, eagles, and vultures soar on warm thermals, while tiny hummingbirds, brilliantly colored toucans, macaws, and parrots flit through wooded glades. Around the coastline the seas are home to awesome sharks, mighty whales, beautiful creatures of the coral reef, and even frolicking penguins.

As night falls in the wild, nocturnal creatures awake from their daytime slumbers to search for food and to fill the darkness with their calls. In vibrant cities, human nightlife is evident everywhere in bars and clubs, as people pour out onto the streets that are pulsating with the rhythms of salsa and reggae or samba and tango …

Enjoy it! This is the glorious spirit of Latin America!

**Opposite:** *Set on a high mountain ridge between two Peruvian peaks, the ancient Inca city of Machu Picchu is often hidden from view beneath shrouds of billowing clouds and mist.*

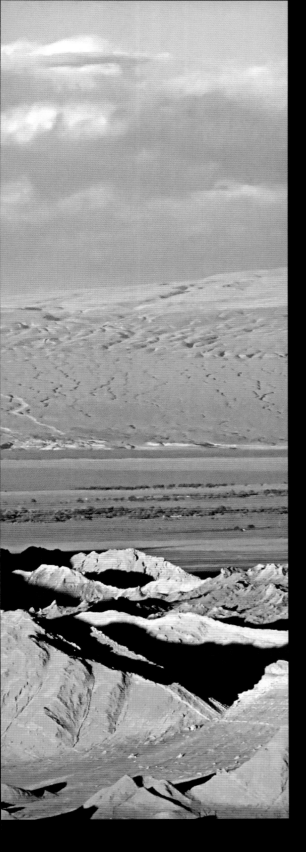

While Latin America encompasses many islands including Caribbean jewels within its boundaries, virtually the entire continent occupies the vast land area that swells like an enormous triangular bag, suspended below the narrow twist of the Panama isthmus. Of the 13 countries that make up South America, Brazil is the largest, claiming over half of all South America's land area and population. An amazing variety of wildlife flourishes here, especially in dense Amazon jungles where bright-eyed jaguars prowl and brilliant parrots soar on colorful wings.

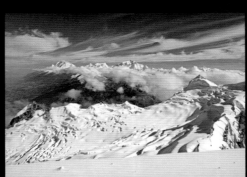

**Left and above:** *Contrasting landscapes include Chile's russet Atacama desert, Patagonian steppes where long-necked guanacos graze, the magnificent wide sweep of Iguaçu Falls, ice-glazed mountains, mighty glaciers, and humid rainforests bright with toucans and parrots.*

# LANDSCAPE AND WILDLIFE

# Coasts and Oceans

The Pacific Ocean was seen for the first time by Europeans early in the 16th century, initially by the Spanish explorer Vasco Núñez de Balboa who crossed the Isthmus of Panama in 1513. It was then navigated by Ferdinand Magellan, who sailed the Pacific from 1519 to 1522 and gave the ocean its name. This is the world's largest ocean—and the deepest. It occupies some 64,186,000sq miles (166,241,000km²), and about one third of the entire world's surface. The North Pacific washes against the shores of Central America and Mexico, while the South Pacific stretches all the way down the western fringe of South America. Only two Latin American nations are 'coastless' (Bolivia and Paraguay), while several face both the Caribbean and the Pacific—especially in the narrow neck of land that links the North and South American land masses.

*Above: Costa Rica's spectacular coastlines provide rich habitats which contain an amazing wealth of marine life and coral reefs, offering the opportunity to catch a glimpse of migrating whales, various dolphin species, sea turtles, and the endangered West Indian manatee.*

*Left: The superb Mayan ruins at Tulum, Mexico, stand on a bluff facing the Caribbean sea and the rising sun. Tulum dates back to around AD 564 but thrived from 1200 to 1521 as a vital link in the Mayas' vast trading network where maritime and land routes converged.*

## Rugged Coasts and Beautiful Beaches

All along the Pacific edge are magnificent rugged coasts. Costa Rica's 802 miles (1290km) of coastline borders the Caribbean and the Pacific, while the seemingly endless Pacific edge of Chile stretches some 2880 miles (4630km) from north to south, with the mighty Andes mountains looming beyond.

Mexico, with its many beautiful beaches, also possesses both Caribbean and Pacific coasts with the beaches at Oaxaca and Sinaloa being famous for their huge waves. The eastern edge of the country wriggles along the Riviera Maya coastline and around the Yucatán peninsula, fringing jungle backdrops and many ancient Mayan sites.

On the western fringe the beautiful Pacific Coast and Puerto Vallarta area are famous for superb beaches, tropical bays, and crystal-clear waters where gray-nosed dolphins swim and often leap in unison in front of the bows of ships.

The Atlantic Ocean, that washes the eastern edge of the Latin American nations, includes the Gulf of Mexico and the romantic Caribbean Sea that is so generously dotted with tropical islands. Then the Atlantic makes a massive 4577 mile (7367km) sweep around the bulbous mass of Brazil. It stretches ever southward as it tumbles against coasts that lie farther south, following past Uruguay to the indented 2899 mile (4665km) eastern coastal rim of Argentina.

## Mosquito Coast

In Central America the Mosquito Coast of southeastern Honduras and Nicaragua was named for the local Miskito Indians, who, in turn, derived their name from the muskets provided by the British and used to resist Spanish colonists. Beyond the beaches lies some of the best-preserved tropical rainforest in the world. The Costa Rica coast includes on its western side Drake Bay, first discovered by Sir Francis Drake in 1579 during his circumnavigation of the globe. Nearby are excellent diving possibilities, with the Isla del Caño Biological Reserve being home to a huge variety of fish, whales, and sharks. In these waters swim barracudas, dolphins, groupers, manta rays, moray eels, sea turtles, sharks, snappers, stingrays, tuna, and whales—including humpback and pilot whales.

*Background: Turquoise seas lap the white sand of Caribbean beaches.*

## Panama

Panama is famous for its amazing canal—built in two stages. Initially construction took place between 1881 and 1888 under the direction of a French company, but work was halted as tropical disease took its toll of the workmen. Later American engineers completed the construction between 1904–1914. Some 51 miles (82km) from its Atlantic entrance to the Pacific terminus in the bay of Panama, it was initially dreamed of back in the 16th century, when the Spanish colonists sought faster and more efficient delivery of the riches of Peru and Ecuador to their home ports. A working plan was drawn up in 1529 but it was not until 1879 that Ferdinand de Lesseps proposed the sea-level canal in the wake of his successful construction of the Suez Canal in Egypt. Today, the Panama canal saves some 18,000 miles (29,000km) of sea travel on a voyage from New York to San Francisco.

For those intent on relaxing or surfing rather than traveling, Panama offers sparkling white sand beaches, palm trees, and soothing breezes. The southern coast faces the Pacific Ocean with its mangrove swamps being home to many different crustaceans—from shrimps to mollusks.

## The Coast of Peru

The Peruvian coastline is, in effect, a long snaking desert hemmed in between the sea to the west and the Andes to the east. Arid deserts and dry coastal ecosystems are interrupted only by the sweep of an occasional cloud-covered valley.

The 200 nautical miles of Peruvian waters are rich in natural resources and feature a wealth of fish, bird, and mammal species, due to the fact that the coastline is influenced by two radically different currents: the cold Humboldt current and the warm El Niño. The cliffs, islands, and beaches here are home to a wide variety of birds, including pelicans, albatrosses, and boobies, while mammals such as sea lions, dolphins, and whales are often seen in the coastal waters.

*Right: Praia do Forte in Salvador de Bahia, Brazil, is a former fishing village which has now become a sophisticated resort. Salvador's beaches include calm inlets, open sea areas with strong waves for surfing—and beaches surrounded by reefs.*

*Inset right: A red beach in Paracas, Peru, set on a beautiful bay and peninsula where fishermen once cast their nets. This has now become a national park—and one of the world's largest marine reserves.*

**Above:** Rio has dozens of beaches including beautiful Itacoatiara beach, host to an international surfing competition. There is also a small cove here with a natural granite pool.

**Top and right:** Morro Branco, Brazil, is renowned for its beige, pink, and russet sand cliffs. In the Labyrinth region, freshwater springs flow from rocky walls, scooped out by erosion.

## Life in the Water

Many creatures make their homes in the waters around the Southern American landmass. The now rare Amazonian manatees, or sea cows, live in the freshwater habitats of the Amazon River and its tributaries. Prehistoric-looking turtles swim in the warm coastal waters and humpback whales congregate off the beaches of Ecuador between June and October to mate. Pacific sea snakes drift on the ocean surface—the highly venomous yellow-bellied sea snake *(Pelamis platurus)* has a special gland under its tongue which secretes salt ingested from the water as it swims, in languid sideward undulations. Its range extends between Ecuador and the Galápagos Islands northward toward Baja California. Fiddler crabs are found in soft sand or mud around the edges of shallow salt marshes from the Gulf of Mexico to South America. Males have one small claw and one enormous claw, which is used as a display to attract a mate. They must work twice as hard to feed themselves as their female counterparts, who are unencumbered by such an unwieldy sex symbol.

These rich waters attract a variety of sharks, from the commonly encountered silky sharks to the strange-looking hammerheads that have eyes on either side at the tips of their T-shaped heads. They are often spotted near Costa Rica. There are whale sharks near Belize—huge fish that eat only plankton yet grow to some 40ft (12.5m) in length, with a mouth that can span up to 5ft (1.5m) in width. The notorious great white shark haunts the waters off Mexico—it is the world's largest known predatory fish, reaching lengths of more than 20ft (6m) and weighing up to 5000lb (2250kg). Shark attacks on humans are rare, despite the great white's fearsome reputation, and such incidents are generally considered to be unintentional, especially in conditions of poor visibility when swimmers or surfboarders may be mistaken for seals or sea lions.

With its upturned nose and large mane, the South American sea lion or Southern sea lion *(Otaria flavescens)* is found on the coasts and islands of Chile, Peru, Uruguay, and Argentina. It hunts for Argentinian hake, anchovies, squid, and octopus—even eating penguins sometimes—but is itself preyed upon by sharks and killer whales.

Penguins include Magellanic and Humboldt penguins in Chile, with Humboldt and Galápagos varieties scuttling around the rocky shores and scooting through the waters off the coast of Peru and around the Galápagos Islands. Southern rockhopper penguins and macaroni penguins breed on offshore islands around Argentina and Chile. The macaroni is the most numerous of all the world's penguins, with an estimated global population of over nine million breeding pairs—all with flamboyant yellow crests.

**Above:** *Magellanic penguins were named for explorer Ferdinand Magellan who spotted them in 1519 on his first voyage around South America's tip. They are 'warm weather' penguins and live on the stormy rocky shores of Argentina and Chile, feeding on squid, krill, sardines, cuttlefish, and crustaceans.*

**Left:** *A sea lion colony in the breathtaking wilderness region beside the Beagle Channel at the southern tip of South America. This 150 mile (240km) long strait was named for the British ship HMS Beagle upon which Charles Darwin voyaged.*

**Opposite:** *A breaching whale—the humpback is famous for its melodious grunts, moans, and haunting songs. It has a pair of pectoral flippers each measuring about one third of its body length, a large expandable throat cavity, and enormous lung capacity, allowing it to remain submerged for over 40 minutes.*

**Background:** In Tierra del Fuego (Patagonia) howling winds shriek above sharp-edged, mist-veiled mountains and barren rocks. Huge ancient glaciers slide imperceptibly into freezing seas where icebergs assume wild shapes and flash with iridescent colors. This is one of the world's most southerly spots, with the archipelago's tip forming Cape Horn. Soon freezing night will descend and then the stars of the Southern Cross will point toward Antarctica.

## Islands Around Latin America

The volcanic Juan Fernández islands off the coast of Chile were home to the castaway sailor Alexander Selkirk for four years in the early 18th century, and his ordeal provided the inspiration for Daniel Defoe's novel *Robinson Crusoe*. Robinson Crusoe Island (formerly Isla Más a Tierra) is the largest island among Chile's sparsely inhabited Juan Fernández archipelago (that also includes Alejandro Selkirk and Santa Clara).

At 3241sq miles (8394km²), Chiloé Island is Chile's second largest island and it is said that the most widely grown potato, *Solanum tuberosum tuberosum*, is indigenous to this spot, having been cultivated here by the local people long before the Spanish arrived.

## The Land of Fire

Tierra del Fuego (the Land of Fire), an archipelago at the southernmost tip of South America, is not the hot place that its name suggests. It was so called after the many glowing fires lit here by the scantily-clad Yamana Indians to help them stay warm in a freezing terrain where glaciers sweep down to the ocean. It belongs jointly to Chile and Argentina. Much of the area is windy, foggy, and wet but, as well as forest, it does encompass steppe and semidesert terrain. The birdlife here includes condors, firecrown hummingbirds, kingfishers, parakeets, owls, and seagulls while roaming below are foxes and llama-like guanacos. Skin from their necks is sometimes flattened and pounded by the locals to make robust soles for shoes. North American beavers, introduced in the 1940s, now wreak havoc in the forests.

*Above:* Bartolomé island, Galápagos, has a fragile lunar-like landscape of lava flows, volcanic tufa, and spatter cones. Tiny lava lizards bask in the sunshine or scurry for cover if disturbed. Out at sea white-tip sharks and stingrays cruise in the shallows as the Pacific surf washes against Pinnacle Rock. The waters here provide rich feeding grounds for a wide variety of species, including brightly colored parrotfish, wrasse, blue-eyed damsels, surgeon fish, and sea urchins.

*Opposite:* The Galápagos islands are home to many vibrant creatures including (clockwise from top left) marine iguanas, the world's only seagoing iguanas who excrete fluid through special glands in their noses to remove excess salt, red-billed tropicbirds that feed on fish and squid, several species of turtles (as well as giant tortoises), and the comical blue-footed boobies whose strange mating dance led the Spaniards to call them bobos (clowns).

## 'Melting Pot' of Species

Life on the Galápagos Islands, set some 600 miles (1000km) to the west of Ecuador's coast, has evolved in virtual isolation for millions of years. They comprise 61 islands and islets, with 13 main islands. Its several volcanoes include Volcan Wolf—at 5600ft (1707m) the highest point in the archipelago. The Galápagos were probably first visited by the Chimu from Peru and later proved an excellent hideout for pirates. The amazing flora and fauna of these islands, flourishing at the confluence of three ocean currents, are a 'melting pot' of marine and terrestrial species and were the catalyst for the formulation of Charles Darwin's Theory of Evolution following his 1835 visit on HMS *Beagle*. Darwin's studies of the variations in the shapes and sizes of the beaks of finches which inhabited the various Galápagos Islands formed the basis of the thesis outlined in his book *On the Origin of Species*, which was published in 1859.

Today its rocky basalt ground vibrates to the dance of blue-footed booby birds as prehistoric-looking marine iguanas sun themselves on black lava rocks along the shore. The Galápagos giant tortoise, the largest living tortoise, is endemic to nine islands here and this slow-moving, hefty creature can enjoy a life expectancy of more than 150 years. Many types of finch flit among the trees, cacti, and mangroves, while tiny Galápagos penguins and flightless cormorants dart through the equatorial waters. Graceful red-billed tropicbirds screech across the sky before settling back on their nests in cliff crevices and burrows. Flamingos flaunt their pink feathers in saltwater lagoons, sifting the shallow water for food. Sea lions lounge and snort on the rocky beaches, while blue, finback, sei, humpback, and minke whales are all to be found in the surrounding ocean together with white-tip, black-tip, tiger, and hammerhead sharks, rays, moray eels, starfish, and sea cucumbers.

## Giant Statues

Easter Island in the southeastern Pacific Ocean is actually in Polynesia but is an overseas territory belonging to Chile, over 2000 miles (3200km) away. This triangle of volcanic rock is one of the most isolated places on the planet and is famous for the 887 monumental stone statues found in Rapa Nui National Park, which represent stylized human heads and torsos. Trees are sparse on the island today but once there were extensive palm forests. Unfortunately these were probably cut down to make the frames that originally supported the massive statues. The loss of its forests led to the rapid decline of the Easter Island civilization.

## Idyllic Islands

Basking in the warm waters of the Caribbean Sea off the north coast of Panama, lies the extensive Bocas del Toro archipelago. This popular tourist destination comprises nine islands, 51 keys, and over 200 islets, set in clear blue waters, with coral reefs and beaches that serve as breeding grounds for many marine species, including manatees and thousands of sea turtles that lay their eggs here between August and November.

A good number of the 7000 islands in the Caribbean are part of Latin America. In 1492, the Italian navigator and explorer Christopher Columbus first set foot in the New World in the Dominican Republic (then Hispaniola). He had discovered not only a whole new continent but a multitude of idyllic islands, which have long been treasured as a place of escape—as indeed they can be, provided the hurricane season is avoided! Many of the Caribbean islands are actually the exposed peaks of an underwater mountain range.

*Right:* With a large flat plain providing easy access to a natural stone quarry, the largest Easter Island statues were erected at Ahu Tongariki. A vast ceremonial platform originally supported 15 statues. Unfortunately, an earthquake in Chile in 1960 triggered a massive tsunami which destroyed the platform and swept the massive figures inland. The site was substantially restored in the 1990s—a task which took five years to complete.

## Creatures of the Caribbean

In the waters of the Caribbean the West Indian manatee grazes on ocean-floor plants while some 3000 humpback whales gather to breed in shallow waters off the north coast of the Dominican Republic. The Caribbean has wonderful coral reefs and the sealife here includes angel fish, barracuda, butterfly fish, parrotfish, porcupine fish, queen trigger fish, and reef sharks. There are bottlenose and spinner dolphins, humpback whales, marlin, and swordfish. The dark shapes of hawksbill, loggerhead, green, and leatherback turtles drift like deep shadows through the turquoise waters. Hundreds of species inhabit both the fringes and banks of islands or offshore barrier reefs, including corals, sponges, worms, mollusks, crabs, and lobsters.

The American crocodile has managed to colonize much of Latin America, its range including Peru and the Caribbean. At night these fearsome creatures, that sometimes reach 20ft (6m) in length, hunt fish, turtles and even take the occasional goat or dog. Rather rarer is the rhinoceros iguana, an endangered species endemic to Hispaniola (Haiti and the Dominican Republic) that has three small horns on its snout, a 'helmeted' head, and a large throat pouch.

Shorebirds include great egrets, American frigate birds, brown pelicans, blue herons, glossy ibis, ruddy ducks, and flamingos. Throughout the Caribbean, palms, rubber trees, tropical fruit, and tobacco plants grow apace and they create safe habitats for a wide variety of birds, including hummingbirds, parrots, woodpeckers, trogons, parakeets, and the endangered white-crowned pigeon. Farther inland, royal palms, coconut palms, Hispaniolan mahogany, West Indian cedars, olives, American muskwood, Creolean pines, ferns, and hundreds of different species of orchid flourish.

## Captivating Cuba

With its sun-battered dusty capital city of Havana, Cuba still conjures up the atmosphere that permeates the novels of Ernest Hemingway, with its aroma of cigars and the sight of wonderful old cars basking in the sun. Cuba has dazzling beaches and an amazing biodiversity that boasts a multitude of different landscapes including coral reefs, mangrove forests, and pristine island wilderness. Some 70,000 nesting Caribbean flamingos strut in the western hemisphere's largest such colony, minute frogs (some barely the size of a fingernail) scramble through the leaf litter of riverine forest—and great clouds of mosquitoes whine above the fetid swamps. The 1.5 million acre (600,000-hectare) Ciénaga de Zapata Biosphere Reserve is Cuba's largest protected area, and one of the most important wetlands in the Caribbean. It is home to many aquatic birds and to more than 3000 Cuban crocodiles (*Crocodylus rhombifer*). These medium-sized reptiles rarely exceed 10.5ft (3.5m) in length and are one of the most threatened crocodile species in the New World because of their small population and restricted distribution.

*Above left:* The hawksbill turtle is most often seen in shallow lagoons and coral reefs where it feeds on its chosen prey, sea sponges. Some of the sponges eaten by the hawksbill are known to be highly toxic and often lethal when eaten by other creatures.

*Above right:* The queen angel fish is a shy, exotic reef-dweller with an electric blue body, blazing yellow tail, and a speckled, blue-ringed spot high on its head which gives the appearance of a regal crown.

*Opposite:* The brown pelican is the only one of seven pelican species that lives along ocean shores rather than inland lakes. It is also the only one that plunges from the air into the water to catch its prey.

*Above: Cuba is home to one of the largest colonies of glorious pink Caribbean flamingos in the western hemisphere. Their preferred habitats are saline lagoons, mudflats, and shallow brackish coastal lakes.*

*Right: A heron flies majestically over a Cuban shore. Many stilt-legged waders patrol the coasts here and the island's prolific birdlife includes little blue herons, tricolored herons, great egrets, reddish egrets, snowy egrets, and cattle egrets. Cuba also boasts the bee hummingbird, the smallest bird in the world.*

# Mighty Rivers and Lakes

The world's greatest river, the Amazon, begins as a glacial stream on a 18,363ft (5597m) high peak called Nevado Mismi in southern Peru. The entire Amazon basin, the largest drainage basin in the world, flows into nine nations, with only about one half of its length (from the east coast of Brazil to the city of Iquitos in Peru) being navigable. One fifth of the world's fresh water runs along the Amazon and with over 1100 tributaries, its average flow of 6 million cu ft (175,000m³) per second translates as 28 billion gallons (ten million tons) of water pouring into the sea every minute—a vast freshwater discharge that dilutes the salinity of the Atlantic for more than 100 miles (160km) offshore. Fed by heavy rainfall, the massive Amazon and its hundreds of tributaries flow past forests and endless jungle—a green mantle often described as the 'lungs of our planet' because the rainforest continuously recycles carbon dioxide into oxygen, producing over 20 percent of the world's supply.

*Above:* The jagged peaks of Mount Cerro Torre (10,280ft/3133m) rise dramatically in Patagonia on the border between Chile and Argentina.

*Left:* The Iguaçu waterfalls tumble between Argentina and Brazil in a rainbow-lit torrent of water and white foam that explodes into the river. A wealth of wildlife lives in the lush vegetation of Iguaçu National Park.

## Where Rivers Flow

Other major rivers include the Negro that rises in the southern highlands of Brazil and then flows southwest into Uruguay. However, the name Río Negro (Black River) variously refers to several waterways in Latin America, including the left tributary of the Uruguay River, the left tributary of the Amazon River, the Río Negro in Patagonia, and one in Chaco Province in Argentina. The Río Negro that has its headwaters in Venezuela forms part of the frontier between Venezuela and Colombia, then enters Brazil to travel east and join the Amazon River, its dark waters making a sharp contrast with the light brown shade of the Orinoco and Amazon Rivers. The Paraná, the second longest river in South America, begins its 3032-mile (4879km) course in east-central Brazil and flows mainly among high plateaus through Paraguay and Argentina. It merges with the Paraguay and Uruguay Rivers before emptying into the Río de la Plata estuary and thence into the Atlantic Ocean. Confusingly, the river's name has also been given to a much shorter river in central Brazil.

The Orinoco River system is one of South America's largest, originating along the southern borders of Venezuela and Brazil, on the western slopes of the Parima Mountains. Its estimated length is some 1700 miles (2740km), making it one of the world's largest river systems. Its giant arc sweeps through Venezuela and enters the Atlantic Ocean near Trinidad. It is home to the Orinoco crocodile and the aggressive cariba piranha, while its river basin is inhabited by indigenous Indian groups. The German naturalist Alexander von Humboldt explored the basin in 1800 and described the pink river dolphins he found there. These friendly, sensitive and intelligent mammals sometimes herd and bank the fish they prey on, often hunting cooperatively with gray dolphins.

Río de la Plata (or River Plate) means Silver River in Spanish and is actually the estuary where the Uruguay and Paraná rivers meet. Its huge mouth gapes 137 miles (220km) wide where it spills into the Atlantic Ocean making it the widest estuary in the world. It delineates part of the border between Argentina and Uruguay and embraces many major ports and capital cities, including Buenos Aires and Montevideo. The estuary was discovered in 1516 by Spanish explorer Juan Díaz de Solís and received its present name from Sebastian Cabot, the Italian-born navigator who was led to believe (wrongly) that the La Plata region contained vast amounts of gold and silver. He searched in vain for untold wealth here.

*Right: The Amazon glows as sunset flames amber with the approach of evening. Some 1100 tributaries empty into this awesome river.*

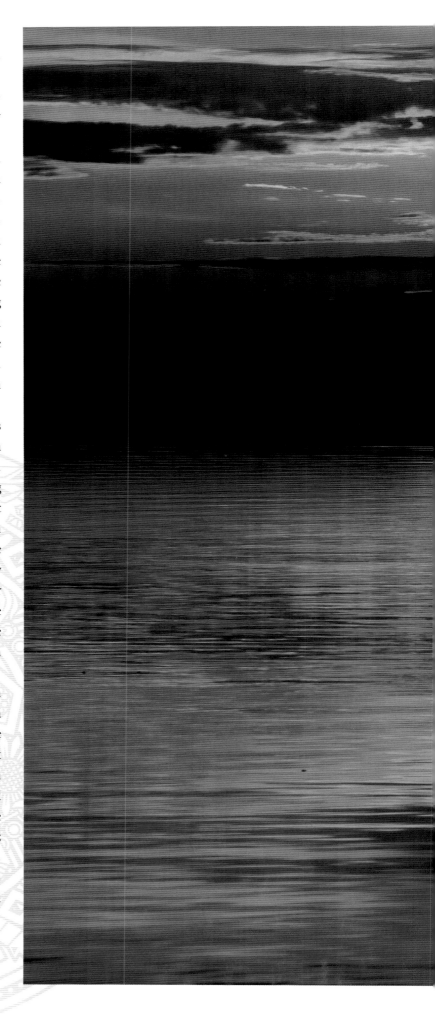

# Rich Waterways

The Río Grande (or Río Bravo) is 1885 miles (3034km) long. Serving as a natural boundary between Mexico and Texas, it marks the point where North America ends and Central America begins. The US and Mexico share the waters of this river under a series of agreements. The most notable of these were signed in 1906 and 1944, and it is administered by the joint US-Mexico Boundary and Water Commission.

The San Juan River is also a natural border, separating Nicaragua and Costa Rica. Prior to the building of the Panama Canal, this river frequently served as a route from the Atlantic to the Pacific Ocean; many African slaves and gold-rush pioneers traveled along its waters and some escaped slaves set up homes here. Tropical rainforests hug shores where freshwater bull sharks, caimans, and turtles swim. Red arrow frogs abound in the thick undergrowth and monkeys clamber in the trees, while countless bird species are found including boat-billed herons, chestnut toucans, cormorants, harpy eagles, great egrets, and small wading birds called jacanas or Jesus birds. Their wide feet allow them to balance on floating vegetation.

The Paraguay River, the principal tributary of the Paraná River is South America's fifth largest. It rises in the Mato Grosso region of Brazil, then crosses Paraguay to join the Paraná near the Argentine border. It is 1584 miles (2550km) long. The Paraguay River is the primary waterway of the Pantanal wetlands that stretch across southern Brazil, northern Paraguay, and parts of Bolivia. This is the world's largest tropical wetlands ecosystem and one which is largely dependent upon waters provided by the Paraguay.

Of course there are countless other rivers in this vast continent, including the Belize that winds along the northern edge of the Maya mountains beside tropical rainforest; the 2100 miles (3380km) stretch of the Madeira (the longest tributary of the Amazon); the Magdalena which is Colombia's main waterway; the São Francisco which at 1964 miles (3160km) is the longest river wholly within Brazil; the Tapajos in central Brazil that pours into the Amazon; the Tocantins that runs north for about 1500 miles (2400km) through Brazil like a central artery—and the Xingu that boasts its very own white-blotched river stingray, *Potamotrygon leopoldi*.

**Above:** The Río Grande (or Río Bravo) which flows from Colorado in the United States to the Gulf of Mexico has, since 1848, marked the boundary between Mexico and the United States.

**Above right:** A caiman in the Pantanal—a region which boasts a caiman ecological refuge in the heart of its southern portion.

**Opposite:** A tortuous river system in Argentina—a swirling pattern that, from above, looks like green marble. Argentina has a total of 6800 miles (10,950km) of navigable waterways, many serving as transportation routes, including the Paraná-Uruguay system, which is navigable for nearly 2000 miles (about 3200km). The great Río de la Plata estuary is formed by the confluence of the Paraná and Uruguay rivers.

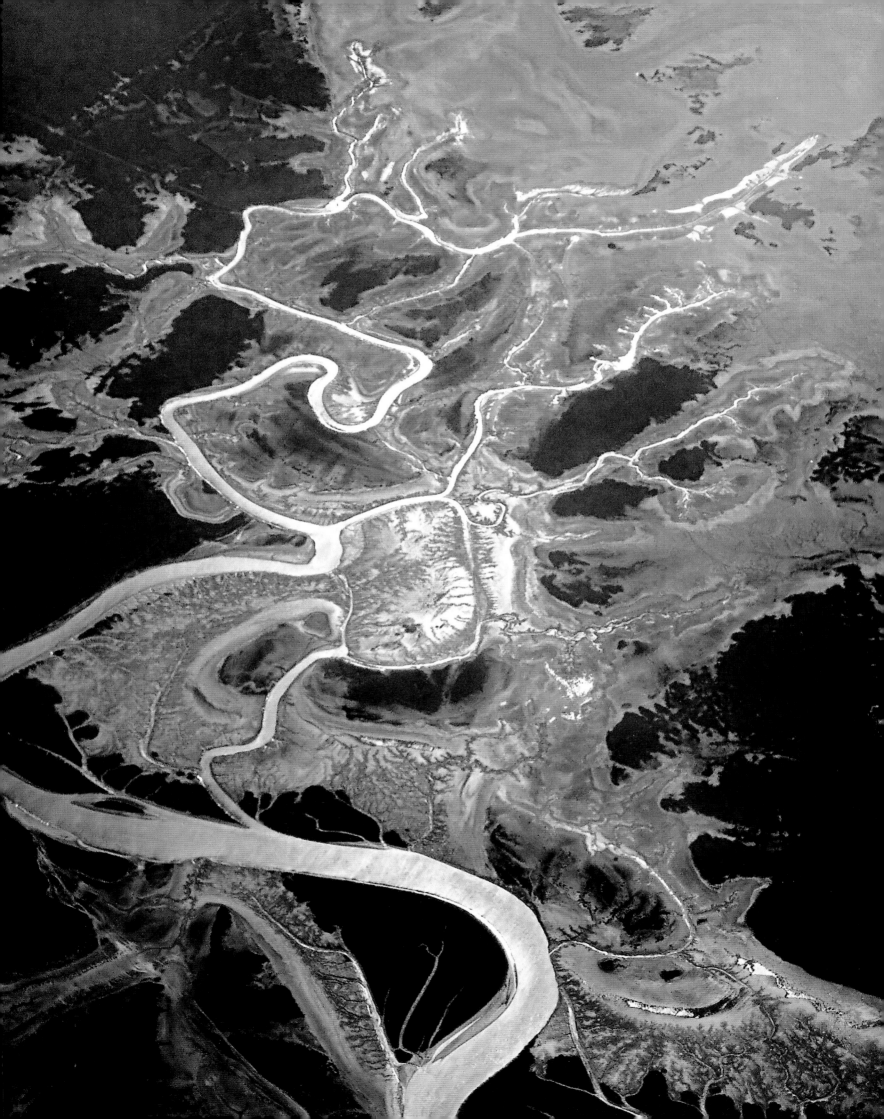

## Fantastic Waterfalls

Rainbows dance in amazing waterfalls throughout Latin America but the globe's tallest free-falling waterfall is the Angel Falls, a simply stunning cascade that tumbles 3212ft (979m), with a clear drop of 2648ft (807m). It plunges down the sheer table mountainside and then drops to the river below—and is some 15 times higher than Niagara Falls. It is found in Canaima National Park in Venezuela.

The falls are named for James Crawford Angel, an adventurous bush pilot who spotted them in 1933 when hunting for gold and returned four years later to land on the flat top of the mountain. His plane nosedived into the marshy ground on landing and stuck fast. There it remained for 33 years. Angel and his companions had to scramble down the mountain and hack their way through thick undergrowth to find their way back to civilization—an ordeal that lasted 11 days. Close to the Angel Falls, but in a remote jungle location, is La Catira, a nonpermanent seasonal waterfall but a mighty one when in full flood.

*Left:* The Angel Falls, the world's highest waterfall, plunges off the edge of a tepui, a table-top mountain in Venezuela. It drops from the Devil's Canyon to cascade in a roaring torrent of water and spray.

*Below:* San Rafael is Ecuador's highest, mightiest waterfall. Surrounded by rainforest it offers (on clear days) views of the active Reventador volcano.

## Thundering Spectacles

One of the globe's most spectacular waterfalls is the incredibly wide sweep of the thundering Iguaçu Falls that gush along the border between Argentina and Brazil. First seen by European eyes when Spanish conquistador, Álvar Núñez Cabeza de Vaca discovered them in 1541, they were not rediscovered by outsiders for another 350 years or so. Viewpoints and walkways offer spectacular vistas and, at one point, the spectator is surrounded by a 260 degree panorama of thundering water. On the border of northern Argentina and southern Brazil, La Garganta del Diablo (the Devil's Throat) is the biggest single falls within the vast Iguaçu Falls complex that hosts between 275 to 350 separate falls depending on seasonal water levels.

The height of the double drop of the Gocta waterfall in Peru is disputed but some claim it to have a 755ft (230m) upper tier and a 1775ft (541m) lower leap. Its existence has only recently been revealed to the outside world and precise measurements remain to be recorded. Unofficially it is listed as the world's fifth tallest. Its name derives from the sound made by monkeys living here. Also in Peru, the recently discovered Yumbilla waterfall is 2937ft (895m) high, the third tallest in the world and the highest in Peru—a country that also boasts the Chinata waterfall (the spring that falls from heaven), which tumbles down approximately 1903ft (580m), and is surrounded by orchids, ferns, moss, and a wealth of luxuriant jungle vegetation.

**Left and above:** *The first European to see the Iguaçu waterfalls was the Spanish conquistador, Álvar Núñez Cabeza de Vaca in 1541. This spectacular vast fan of tumbling water has featured in many movies including the James Bond film* Moonraker *(1979),* The Mission *(1986),* Miami Vice *(2006) and* Indiana Jones and the Kingdom of the Crystal Skull *(2008).*

## Smoke and Ice

The Waterfall of Smoke (Cachoeira da Fumaça) is Brazil's second largest. Here the force of the wind turns the water into vapor—to beautiful effect as its name implies. Upriver are the 1197ft (365m) Cachoeira do Aracá falls, Brazil's highest (discovered only in 2001) at an altitude of 4921ft (1500m), set in a remote but beautiful mountainous region on the Venezuelan border. Also in Brazil is Caracol waterfall, where a 427ft (130m) cascade plummets over basaltic rock formations, and the Andorinhas (Swallows) waterfall which flows like a stairway, cascading down to natural pools where swallows gather in summer.

Chile boasts the Cascada de Ventisquero Colgante (Hanging Glacier Falls) with a 1600ft (487m) drop as icy waters pour across the rocks in Queulat National Park, Patagonia. Chihuahua state in Mexico (Land of the Great Canyons) offers the 1486ft (453m) Piedra Volada (Flying Stone) waterfall, discovered in 1994 in Copper Canyon and the tallest in Mexico, plus the 812ft (246m) Basaseachic fall tumbling down to thick pine tree forests, and the beautiful wide-sweeping Cusarare waterfalls.

Other magnificent cascades in Latin America include the 2000ft (610m) high Cuquenan Falls in Venezuela, set amid a landscape of flat-topped table mountains. These drop in an initial awe-inspiring gush and then sweep on to plunge down yet again.

*Below:* Several cascades tumble over a wide craggy ledge in Venezuela, with the roar of the water adding to the drama of the spectacle.

*Opposite:* This wide sweep of tumbling water is also in Venezuela, a country famous for its many waterfalls, often hidden in deep jungle.

## Special Lakes

Latin America does not have a particularly great number of large lakes. Maracaibo in Venezuela is South America's biggest, a brackish body of water covering 5150sq miles (13,300km$^2$) while at 12,500ft (3810m), Lake Titicaca is South America's second largest and the world's highest navigable lake, set amid the lofty Andes astride the border between Peru and Bolivia. Some 25 rivers or so empty their waters here where ruins on the shore and on the lake's islands testify to an ancient culture. According to tradition, the legendary founders of the Inca dynasty were sent down to Earth here by the sun god.

The largest lake in Central America is Lake Nicaragua, covering 3330sq miles (8624km$^2$). It is one of the world's biggest freshwater lakes. It lies on the border between Nicaragua and Costa Rica. Freshwater bull sharks, sawfish, tarpon, and swordfish live here. It is connected to the Caribbean Sea via the San Juán River, which provided the means of entry both for the Spanish conquistadores—who founded the city of Granada on the lakeshore—and for sharks that leap the rapids like giant salmon. Near to the port of Granada is an archipelago of more than 350 tropical islets.

The damming of the Río Negro near Paso de los Toros, Uruguay, created a vast reservoir, Rincón del Bonete (also known as the Gabriel Terra or Río Negro reservoir). At 4000sq miles (10,360km$^2$), this is South America's largest artificial lake. Bolivia's windswept salt lake, Laguna Verde (Green Lagoon), set beside the Licancabur volcano, is an amazing turquoise hue, its stunning color caused by sediments containing copper and other minerals in the water.

Chile's Lake District is spectacular with deep blue lakes lying below the snow-capped Andes and surrounded by larch forests, rivers, waterfalls, hot springs, and six volcanoes, with Villarrica the highest at 9340ft (2847m). Among the dozens of lakes in this area are 12 major bodies of water as well as numerous fjords and islands dotted with pretty wooden houses featuring high-pitched roofs and ornate balconies.

*Above right: At Bolivia's Laguna Verde high concentrations of lead, sulfur, arsenic, and calcium create a shimmering blue-green sheet of water.*

*Opposite left: Upsala glacier—one of 13 that descend from the Patagonian continental ice field to flow into the Viedma and Argentino lakes.*

*Opposite right: 41 islands in Lake Titicaca are revered as sacred with the largest, Isla del Sol, regarded as home of the supreme Inca god Inti.*

*Following pages: Chile's Torres del Paine National Park has many lakes.*

## Lake Dwellers

The South American silver catfish *(Rhamdia quelen)* is a bottom-dwelling species that is widely distributed in the lakes, reservoirs, and rivers of Latin America where the waters are also home to many dangerous creatures, such as alligators, caimans, electric eels, and gigantic anacondas—boa constrictors that live in the swamps and rivers of dense tropical forests, especially in Venezuela, and which can grow to 23ft (7m) in length. The notorious sharp-toothed piranha fish resides here too, but it is really vicious only when circumstances drive it to compete for space and prey. In fact, some species are vegetarian, using their fearsome teeth to crack open nuts that fall into the water. Creatures with a rather more peaceful disposition include otters, pelicans, and the famous pink and gray river dolphins.

# Awe-inspiring Mountains

Impressive mountain ranges rise to towering heights in many Latin American nations. In Central America, mountains thread their way through much of the interior. Mexico's prominent mountain ranges—the Sierra Madre Occidental and the Sierra Madre Oriental—meet up near Mexico City to form the sharp-peaked Sierra Madre del Sur. The Pico de Orizaba, Mexico's highest peak, is a dormant volcano that rises 18,580ft (5636m). It has not erupted since a fairly vigorous burst of activity in the 16th and 17th centuries.

## Impressive Highlands

The Guiana Highlands stretch from southern Venezuela to the tip of Brazil to form a mountainous tableland, bounded by the Orinoco and Amazon river basins. Often the crystalline rock formations yield gold and diamonds. The range encompasses many strange table mountains (or tepuis), which form when wind and rain erode softer rocks, leaving curious formations and flat tops often crowned by beds of moss.

*Above:* A sunset tints Alpamayo's peak in Peru's Cordillera mountains.

*Left:* Cerro Torre in Los Glaciares National Park in the Patagonian Andes. Here jagged peaks thrust high above the slow slide of the mighty glacier as ice chunks topple into the turquoise water below.

## Magnificent Landscapes

These awe-inspiring table mountains have inspired many tales of magic and adventure, including Sir Arthur Conan Doyle's novel *The Lost World*, published in 1912. There are more than 100 tepuis in the Canaima National Park (a UNESCO World Heritage Site) in southeastern Venezuela as well as some of the world's most spectacular waterfalls.

The Brazilian Highlands is a huge elevated region that covers much of eastern, southern, and central Brazil, offering magnificent landscapes with peaks soaring up to 7365ft (2245m) surrounding awe-inspiring gorges and ravines, waterfalls, cliffs, and rocky outcrops. Their Atlantic Plateau section runs all along Brazil's eastern coast. Once almost completely covered by rainforest, today only some 7 percent remains of what was once one of the globe's richest areas of biodiversity with fine hardwoods and rich vegetation that provides cover for jaguars, cougars, tapirs, and monkeys.

## Mountain Ranges

There are three major mountain ranges in the province of Córdoba in central Argentina: the Sierras Chicas to the north, the Sierras Grandes to the south (where dams raised along the Sierras Grandes valleys have created a series of beautiful lakes), and the Sierras de Comechingones in the southwest. The ancient Sierras de Córdoba, formed in Paleozoic times, have been extensively eroded since that era. They surround salt lakes (the largest being Salinas Grandes) that absorb most of the water flow from the mountains—and alpine grasslands. Today these heights are a favored destination for many tourists who enjoy rock climbing and paragliding in the company of swooping soaring birds.

Bolovia's Cordillera Real is a subrange of the Andes that lies just northeast of La Paz. This granite range of fold mountains boasts six summits higher than 19,700ft (6000m) with Illimani (meaning 'golden eagle') being the highest peak.

*Above:* Auyantepui (Devil's Mountain) is the famous table-top mountain in Venezuela from which the Angel Falls plummet, dropping from a cleft near the summit. It encompasses a vast plateau of some 251sq miles (650km²) and has a peak nearly 9850ft (3000m) high.

*Opposite:* The ice-draped summits of the Cordillera Blanca range in Peru—here the most magnificent ice-fluted peaks tower above a glacial wilderness dimpled with turquoise lakes and, when the snows do retreat, beautiful flowering alpine meadows.

# The Andes

Notwithstanding the splendor of these peaks, it is the main thrust of the mighty Andes that undoubtedly overshadows all others so far as South American mountains are concerned. This massive tooth-sharp range extends all the way from Panama down to the tip of South America and is around 4500 miles (7240km) long—a stunning mixture of ice and fire, with many amazing active volcanoes as well as vast glacial ice sheets. The Andes is the longest exposed mountain range in the world and the highest range outside Asia. It encompasses several other individually named mountain ranges (the most important being the Cordillera Oriental and Cordillera Occidental) as well as subranges, ridges, and many sharp branches. The condor *(Vultur gryphus)*—a national symbol in Argentina, Bolivia, Chile, Colombia, Ecuador, and Peru— soars majestically above Andean peaks with the highest being Aconcagua in Argentina at 22,841ft (6962m), the topmost peak in the western hemisphere.

Along this great sweep of mountains dramatic changes of climate and terrain are experienced. The predominant landscape ranges from lush rainforests to snowy peaks. The hotter regions closest to the Equator are found in the northern areas, where rainforests thrive in a generally humid rainy climate. The southern stretches, near to the Antarctic, are much colder and less-populated while, in between these two extremes, is a milder central region where the largest bromeliad in the world, *Puya raimondii*, survives at elevations above 13,000ft (4000m). This extraordinary plant takes up to 70 years to reach maturity and produce flowers, and sometimes lives for more than a century. In some regions, gold, silver, and copper are mined and this activity can threaten the local environment but, generally, the Andes are home to an incredibly rich range of flora and fauna.

*Right:* Mount Aconcagua (Mendoza province, Argentina) is the highest mountain in the Americas and the world's highest outside Asia. It rises 22,841ft (6962m) but, despite this awe-inspiring elevation, the climb to the summit by the northern route is technically relatively easy. The Polish Glacier creates an excellent, if slightly more difficult, scenic route to the summit but the south face climb is very difficult.

*Left: Mountain peaks glisten white with pristine snow in Peru's Cordillera Blanca. Melting snow from the Cordillera Blanca provides Peru with the majority of its water supplies, while some 80 percent of Peru's power comes from hydroelectricity.*

*Top left: The impressive 19,511ft (5947m) peak of Alpamayo in the Cordillera Blanca, a perfectly sculpted pyramid of snow and ice.*

*Top right: A sure-footed guanaco pauses to survey the amazing mountain scenery in Torres del Paine National Park, Patagonia.*

*Above left: The Andes form the world's longest exposed mountain range, creating a continuous chain along the west coast of South America.*

*Above right: Mount Fitz Roy in Los Glaciares, Argentina, rises 11,171ft (3405m) high above a landscape of imposing peaks and glaciers.*

## Andean Wildlife

Llamas, alpacas, guanacos (camel-like animals with thick neck skin that protects them during mating-time squabbles), and their close relatives vicuñas live in open grassy pastures at high altitude. The Andes are also home to the nocturnal, silvery-gray, dense-haired chinchillas that bound, cling, and scramble over the rocky terrain in their nightly forages for plants, roots, and grasses. Once their soft fur was used to make coats and millions of chinchillas were killed for their pelts. They nearly became extinct in the 1940s but now this endangered secretive creature is protected by law.

The predatory cougar *(Puma concolor)*, which stalks the mountains for prey, has some 40 different names, including mountain lion, cuguacuarana, and puma (puma is the native Peruvian name). It cannot roar but can hiss, growl, purr, and make whistling noises. It is a formidable and fast hunter, often pursuing large rodents like capybara, and is notable in being able to leap across distances of up to 40ft (12m).

Another large mammal found in the cloud forests of the Andes, in Colombia and Ecuador, is the solitary mountain tapir *(Tapirus pinchaque)* which has a dark woolly coat and a long probing prehensile nose. Mountain tapirs are generally nocturnal and spend long hours foraging along well-worn trails, snouts to the ground as they look for juicy fruit, berries, and leaves. They seek out natural salt licks to satisfy their need for essential minerals. Like all tapirs, they enjoy wallowing and swimming in water.

Spectacled bears *(Tremarctos ornatus)*—so called because of their distinctive face markings—are the only surviving bears in South America and are found along the slopes of the Andes mountains from Venezuela to Peru. They are excellent climbers and even young individuals enjoy scrambling up trees, rocks, and cliffs as their mothers keep a watchful eye on their progress. Spectacled bears often make their homes in dens in high-altitude Andean cloud forests above 6500ft (2000m), where they include epiphytic bromeliads in their varied diet of roots, leaves, shoots, berries, rodents, and carrion.

The 'conventional' (but still absolutely beautiful) woolly monkey *(Lagothrix* spp.) is found in Brazil, Columbia, Ecuador, and Venezuela but the yellow-tailed woolly monkey *(Oreonax flavicauda)* is an extremely rare species found only in Peru's western Andes, in mountain cloud forests at elevations up to 8200ft (2500m). Before being rediscovered in 1974, it was considered extinct.

More than 600 reptile species thrive in the Tropical Andes, including snakes and river turtles. The Tropical Andes stretch from western Venezuela to northern Chile and Argentina and include large parts of Colombia, Ecuador, Peru, and Bolivia. It is also the most important region in the world for amphibians, with around 980 species, of which some 670 are endemic. The best-known amphibians here are the brightly colored poison-dart frogs, some of which are among the most poisonous organisms on Earth. In the cooler southern regions of the Andes, reptiles are less common but examples include the giant toad and Andean iguana.

In the skies above, black condors ride on mountain thermals. The western hemisphere's largest flying land bird, the condor often features in Latin American folklore and mythology. Here too soar Andean eagles, dwarfing those few hummingbird species that can survive at altitudes above 13,100ft (4000m), while their lower-dwelling relatives haunt the humid Andean cloud forests. Among the wide variety of birds seen along the Andes are flamingos and plate-billed mountain toucans (*Andigena laminirostris*)—gorgeously colored and sporting huge beaks, these magnificent creatures are found at elevations approaching 9000ft (2750m) in Ecuador, Colombia, and Peru.

The vibrant scarlet or brilliant orange Andean cock-of-the-rock (*Rupicola peruviana*) is Peru's national bird and is renowned for its impressive display dances. Sometimes several dozen males will gather to perform their exuberant mating rituals in a place called a 'lek,' posturing and flourishing their crests. Another spectacular bird, the resplendent quetzal (*Pharomachrus mocinno*) is found from southern Mexico to western Panama. It was often depicted in ancient times as this bird was the most sacred symbol of the Mayas, associated with the Toltec feathered serpent god Quetzalcoatl, while the Mexican Aztecs allowed only royalty or the nobility to don its long exotic tail plumes.

*Background:* Salmon-colored flamingos wade through the shallow waters at Uyuni in western Bolivia where there are expansive salt flats and lakes tinted red by algae.

*Below left:* The vivid color and dramatic markings of this poison-arrow frog from Peru serve as a warning to potential predators.

*Below:* The snows of Bolivia's highest peak, Mount Sajama, provide year-round water for alpacas and a small community of herders.

# Fiery Volcanoes

Latin America has many volcanoes, sitting as it does above the eastern Pacific's Nazca Plate—this is one of the world's most active tectonic regions. It is also the longest of any continental volcanic region with 204 volcanoes. It is second only to Japan in the number of volcanoes with dated eruptions. Some are dormant, of course, but many others are active—occasionally with tragic results. The 1985 eruption of the Nevado del Ruiz volcano in Colombia left 22,000 people dead and 6000 families homeless.

*Right: A volcanic peak in Bolivia's Cordillera range. High above the Andes, soaring on the thermals, majestic black condors can often be seen; they are the western hemisphere's largest flying land birds. Elusive pumas, jaguars, tapirs, and giant anteaters also haunt the Cordillera heights.*

*Below: Close to Mexico City, Popocatépetl is the northern hemisphere's highest active volcano. In 1994 an eruption caused gas and ash emissions to spread up to 16 miles (25km) away. In 2001 pyroclastic flows (fluidized hot gas, ash, and volcanic rocks) caused glacial melting here.*

*Opposite below: An aerial view of Chimborazo, the highest Ecuadorian Andes summit. Due to its close proximity to the bulge of the Equator this stratovolcanic peak is the farthest point from the center of the Earth.*

## Smoking Mountains

Close to Mexico City, Mexico, the delightfully named Popocatépetl (its Aztec name means 'Smoking Mountain') rises 17,890ft (5426m) into the heavens. It is a massive glacier-clad stratovolcano, and is one of the most active volcanoes in Mexico. Plumes of steam and ash often rise from its steep-walled crater, evidence that this puffing giant has given vent to many eruptions—recorded since the pre-Columbian era when Aztec manuscripts described them—often exhibiting dramatic pyroclastic flows.

Most Latin American volcanoes are located along the western edge of the continent and its Pacific rim and they are found in Colombia, Ecuador, the Galápagos Islands, Peru, Chile, and Bolivia, with some in Argentina. The world's highest active volcano is the massive Ojos del Salado, rising to 22,614ft (6893m) on the Chile-Argentina border. It contains a permanent crater lake situated some 20,965ft (6390m) up on its eastern side; this is thought to be the world's highest lake. Chile is a good place to tour volcanoes, as it has the region's largest number of historically active volcanoes, with 36 (ranking it fifth among nations, behind Russia's 52 and ahead of Iceland's 18). Ecuador, the region's smallest country in terms of population and area, is next in the volcano league table, with 16 listed.

## Active Volcanoes

The most active volcano in Costa Rica is the 5436ft (1657m) Arenal in the Arenal Volcano National Park. After some four centuries of dormancy, it erupted in 1968 and the explosion destroyed the town of Arenal and killed 87 people. It still has minor eruptions, sometimes as frequently as every 5-10 minutes, and is one of the most active volcanoes in the western hemisphere as its pyramid-shaped cone spouts constant eruptions of lava from its central crater.

In Nicaragua, a visit to the colonial city of León often involves a tour of the UNESCO World Heritage Site of León Viejo, the original town that was destroyed by an earthquake in 1610 and then buried by volcanic ash when Momotombo volcano erupted the following year. In the local Indian language, Momotombo means 'active and close to waters,' referring to Lake Managua which lies below the 4100ft (1250m) cone. Nearby, in San Jacinto village, there are boiling mud holes which sometimes eject small rocks in the air as steam is continuously emitted from the craters. Also in Nicaragua, Cerro Negro volcano rises 2388ft (728m). It is Central America's youngest volcano, born in 1850, and it is still very active, with ash and gas clouds rising from its crater and vents as well as rock and lava flows. In 1999 Cerro Negro began erupting a week after 2000 people had been killed by a mudslide originating from nearby Casita volcano.

In 2008, close to the Ecuador border, Colombia's Galeras volcano erupted. Thousands of people were safely evacuated while Galeras spewed ash 5 miles (8km) high into the sky and red-hot lava cascaded down its slopes. Several other volcanoes in Ecuador have been active recently—including Tungurahua (Throat of Fire) that spouted vigorous ash eruptions and steam plumes in January 2008. The generally volatile volcanic scene in Chile includes Chaitén volcano which erupted violently in May 2008 after a dormant period lasting some 9000 years.

**Left:** Cerro Negro volcano in the Cordillera de los Maribios mountain range in Nicaragua consists of a dark cinder cone which contrasts with the surrounding green vegetation and gives rise to its name, which means black hill.

**Opposite below:** Close to San José, Poás is a much-visited Costa Rican volcano. It is believed to have been erupting for some 11 million years. Luxuriant forests surround the craters.

**Below:** A streak of hot lava gleams on Arenal's flanks, one of the world's ten most active volcanoes. The flow can change direction without warning but park rangers here observe volcanic activity carefully and advise visitors as to the safety of trails.

# The Great Forests

In a continent rich in jungle habitat, there are densely wooded subtropical lowlands in Argentina and Costa Rica, further richly forested areas in Mexico, Peru, and Venezuela and, just south of the Amazon River basin, the Humid Chaco, a heavily forested lowland with thornbrush jungle and quebracho trees, long exploited for their extremely hard durable wood and useful tannins. Parts of this region are so thickly covered in vegetation that they are locally called *El Impenetrable*.

## A Wealth of Wildlife

The biodiversity of Mexico's forests is outstanding. In particular, they are rich in pines and contain 50 percent of the world's species of this tree and 135 different oak species. Some 80 percent of the forests belong to local communities but many are vanishing fast.

*Above: Splayed orange toes help the red-eyed tree frog cling to branches and leaves in Costa Rica's rainforests. If disturbed when dozing, the frogs will flash open their bright red eyes to scare away predators.*

*Left: Lush vegetation, mosses, and ferns create a gleaming emerald world in Costa Rica's rainforests. They are home to hummingbirds, orchids, bromeliads, many entwining plants, and countless insects. Beautiful cloud forests cover the higher volcanic slopes, often cloaked in dense fog.*

## The Maya Forest

The Maya Forest forms the heart of the Yucatán Peninsula, covering more than 6 million acres (2.4 million hectares) from Mexico's Caribbean coast across Belize and into Guatemala. Here are found 95 mammal, 45 reptile, 18 amphibian, 112 fish, and 400 bird species. During peak winter migration, some five billion birds pass through the area, while residents include black-billed cuckoos, crested guans, great curassows, jabiru storks, king vultures, and scarlet macaws.

There are endangered animals too, like the giant anteater *(Myrmecophaga tridactyla)* which has stiff straw-like hair and a long bristling tail. It can rip open a termite hill with a sharply clawed paw and slide its tubular snout into the opening, probing its long sticky tongue deep into the heart of the colony to trap the insects. It can consume up to 30,000 ants and termites in a single day. Mother anteaters carry their single offspring on their backs.

Howler monkeys (various *Alouatta* species) fill the forests with their distinctive barking whoops and roars. These are among the world's loudest land animals and their calls can be heard up to 3 miles (5km) away. As they swing through the canopy to find juicy leaves and fruit, they keep a wary eye open for any predatory harpy eagles soaring above.

Five species of large cat prowl through the Maya Forest— jaguar and jaguarundi (a wild cat with short legs that resembles a large otter and is sometimes called otter cat), puma, ocelot, and the petite tigrillo or oncilla *(Leopardus tigrinus)* that has an exquisitely beautiful coat and roams in high mountain forests—it is sometimes seen at altitudes of 14,750ft (4500m) right up to the mountain snowline.

## Ancient Evergreen Forests

In Mexico's Lacandon rainforest region there are tropical and montane rainforests, cloud forests, semi-deciduous tropical forests, savannahs, pine-oak forests, seasonally flooded forests, gallery forests, and open wetlands. Here some 4000 species of vascular plants thrive and there are plentiful timber, fruit, and gum trees—sometimes the leaves of palm trees serve as roofing material for the huts of local villagers. Illegal loggers often try to exploit the natural resources of this 10,000-year-old evergreen forest reserve, which is an important haven for vast colonies of orange and gold monarch butterflies—some of which fly up to 50 miles (80km) a day and cover an amazing total of 2000 miles (3220km) on their fragile wings to reach their winter destination here.

**Left:** *Some dense rainforests survive in southeastern Mexico along the Gulf of Mexico. These are the New World's most northerly tropical rainforests, and are home to a great diversity of plants and animals. Their continued existence, however, is threatened by illegal felling of timber for fuel and land clearance for agriculture.*

**Top:** *Jaguars once roamed from the Grand Canyon to Argentina but today habitat loss and illegal hunting means that this magnificent species is endangered throughout its greatly reduced range.*

**Above:** *Scarlet macaws are among the most magnificent birds, often flying in pairs above the evergreen forest canopy in the humid tropics. They may live for up to 75 years but 30 to 50 years is more typical.*

## Cloud Forests

In Central and South America's tropical and subtropical mountainous regions, cooler temperatures on the mountain slopes cause clouds to form. Such stretches of evergreen mountain cloud forests can be found from Panama to northern Argentina and here the forests are almost permanently shrouded in mist. In the Andean humid forest, hot equatorial air from the Pacific Ocean meets the steep slopes of the Andes and then, as it rises, it cools and bathes the mountains with moisture and clouds. There are cloud forests in the Caribbean too. Wherever they occur, the trees are generally 50–65ft (15–20m) tall at lower elevations but, higher up the slopes, they remain shorter and mossier.

The countless birds that live in this habitat include yellow-eared parrots, great white egrets, turkey vultures, mustached antpittas (small insect-eating birds), plate-billed mountain toucans, plus soaring kites, eagles, falcons, and hawks. The nighttime forests are haunted by barn owls, mottled owls, screech owls, and nightjars. These humid cloud forests are also home to wonderful mammals, such as Andean spectacled bears, deer, foxes, and pumas.

## Bird Paradise

In Monteverde in Costa Rica the rainforests feature majestically tall trees festooned with orchids, bromeliads, and ferns, while the spectacular Monteverde Cloud Forest Reserve has beautifully wind-sculptured elfin woodlands on exposed ridges. There are deep gorges, crystal-clear streams, rapids, and waterfalls. Wildlife in the reserve includes jaguars, pumas, ocelots, and Baird's tapirs, which roam through the thick vegetation and mists. Some 450 species of bird have been recorded here and they include superb emerald toucanets and the three-wattled bellbird which has thin worm-like wattles of skin that dangle from the base of its bill and throat as it makes loud metallic honks to its mate. Bare-necked umbrella birds have inflatable wattles to amplify their humming calls. Elusive (and aptly named) resplendent quetzals are found here—they are considered to be among the world's most beautiful birds with their vibrantly colored plumage and iridescent green tail feathers. These beautiful birds are poor fliers and instead they hop through the forest vegetation searching for the fruit, berries, lizards, and insects on which they feed.

*Right: In Costa Rica, La Fortuna waterfall plummets through dense jungle.*

**Above:** Its brilliant plumage and enormous brightly colored bill make the toucan one of the most easily recognizable inhabitants of the tropical forests of Latin America.

**Right:** Some 50 hummingbird species live in Costa Rica. Microscopic feather-tip structures create their dazzling iridescent colors when light strikes them.

**Far right:** As spectacular as its name suggests, the resplendent quetzal was considered divine by pre-Columbian Central American civilizations.

**Opposite:** The verdant rainforest vibrates with the insect-like call of poison-dart frogs, rasping cicadas and whistling wrens and antbirds as afternoon cloudbursts freshen the humid air.

# Life in the Forests

In Peru there are mighty cloud forests and lush lowland jungles where waterways, such as the immense chocolate-colored Manu River, meander and sometimes form crystal-clear oxbow lakes. In these remote forests thousands of species of plants and animals thrive. Reptiles sun themselves on riverside beaches while monkeys busily forage for food in the trees and black caimans rise from the depths of lakes in late afternoon to begin their nocturnal search for prey. Heavy barrel-shaped capybaras *(Hydrochoerus hydrochaeris)* potter on slightly webbed feet through dense vegetation near rivers and pools—sometimes diving in and staying cool underwater for as long as five minutes. It is believed that the ancient ancestors of these pig-sized rodents were bigger than today's grizzly bears! Amphibious giant otters *(Pteronura brasiliensis)* swim deftly along rivers, hunting for catfish, piranhas, and other fish and crabs. True to their name, males may grow up to 6ft (1.8m) in length. Over 1000 bird species are found in Peru including colorful parrots and vivid macaws that gather on riverbanks to feed on clay 'licks' to supplement their usual seed-and-fruit diet with vital minerals and salts.

The scale and impact of the Amazonian rainforest is truly breathtaking, forming an emerald and deep-green spread of lush forest which follows the Amazon valley to cover an area of about 2.3 million sq miles (6 million km²). An incredible wealth of wildlife thrives here in both conventional 'jungle' rainforest and in higher altitude cloud forests.

***Above:*** *A rainbow arches over the oxbow Sandoval Lake in Puerto Maldonado, Peru, where rivers are the means of navigating through the dense jungle.*

***Left:*** *Mist veils the green luxuriant Andes cloudforest. Epiphytes, lichens, and ferns thrive in humid equatorial conditions enjoyed by spectacled bears, howler and woolly monkeys, and a wide variety of birds.*

# The Amazon Rainforest

Brazil is host to some 60 percent of the Amazon forest, but this green expanse ignores boundaries and also flows into Bolivia, Colombia, Ecuador, Peru, and Venezuela. The forest is the world's richest biological 'reservoir.' It contains a veritable cornucopia of species with some 50 to 200 different tree species per 2.5 acres (1 hectare), compared with an average of just ten species in temperate woodlands. It is estimated that around 2500 separate tree species are to be found in Amazonia. It has also been proposed that one in five of all the birds in the world live in the Amazon rainforests … not to mention over 40,000 identified plant species, although there are likely to be many thousands more still to be discovered. Here too are some 2.5 million species of insects, including 7500 species of butterflies.

Many trees grow as tall as 200ft (60m) and rely on huge buttress roots to anchor them into the decaying organic undergrowth and the shallow soil that has its nutrients leached away by rainfall. Dense rainforest is a top-heavy ecosystem with its true riches found high in the canopy that is studded with wild flowers among the tangle of woody lianas, vines, creepers, and festoons of epiphytes (plants that grow upon, or attached to, other living plants). To avoid the prevailing shade of the forest floor many scramble high into the canopy for light.

**Above:** *Lianas are woody vines rooted at ground level; they use trees for vertical support and as a convenient route toward precious light and air. Some lianas form bridges between various canopy sections, linking forest patches, looping over gaps and giving animals and insects a means to traverse higher zones of the forest.*

**Opposite:** *This entwined mass of growth looks almost like a mythical tree monster. In the Amazonian rainforest intricate structures mingle and entwine. Some plant combinations may be beneficial, with both species growing to maturity in symbiotic harmony, while others, like the strangler fig, are parasites that may ultimately kill their unfortunate host.*

# Rainforest Flora

Some epiphytes take advantage of ant nests as germination sites for seeds and as a source of nutrients, while in a beneficial symbiosis their roots provide a stable base upon which ants can build their nests. Other epiphytes trap organic debris in 'baskets' formed of aerial roots and take up their nutrients from this humus. Epiphytes include algae, mosses, fungi, ferns, lichens, orchids, and bromeliads—some of which trap water in small pools formed by their tightly overlapping leaf bases which offer a home to tiny frogs and salamanders. A study of plants in Ecuador discovered over 300 distinct species taking advantage of this unusual adaptation, many being bromeliads. Over 1000 species of frogs are found in the Amazon basin, mostly up in the trees, where they enjoy the high humidity and can escape from the many hungry predators that lurk in the water and on the ground.

This wealth of trees and plants includes gigantic Brazil nut trees *(Bertholletia excelsa)* that tower up to 160ft (49m) with their spreading branches and flowers providing habitats and food for numerous forest creatures including the agouti, a rodent with sharp, chisel-like teeth strong enough to split open the nuts' hard seed cases. To reproduce, flowering Brazil trees rely on orchid bees that visit them while collecting nectar from orchids growing nearby and in the process carry pollen from tree to tree so fertilizing the flowers. Sometimes strangler figs creep along the trunks, stealing water and nutrients from the tree through its bark and eventually wrapping tight around their host until the tree dies, and the fig remains like a ghostly monument to the host tree's former glory.

In the shallow oxbow lakes and lagoons of the Amazon River basin, the most magnificent and largest of all aquatic plants grows—the giant Amazon water lily, *Victoria amazonica* with flat, dish-like leaves that sometimes exceed 7ft (2m) in diameter. The flowers are up to 16in (40cm) wide and are white the first night that they open but then shade to pink after a day or two.

*Right: The strangler fig is the common name for a number of tropical plant species, particularly of the genus* Ficus *but also including banyans and unrelated vines. They all share a common habit of 'strangling' the trees on which they grow, as they compete for light in the dense rainforests of the Amazon, often eventually killing their supportive hosts.*

*Opposite top: Miniature orchids like this delicate epiphytic* Lepanthes *have incredibly tiny flowers that may be only 0.11–0.15in (3–4mm) across. The flower pictured grows in the rainforests of Costa Rica but* Lepanthes *species are found from Mexico to as far south as Bolivia.*

## Kill or Cure

Amid all these riches, the indigenous peoples of Amazonia naturally use many forest plants as sources of food, fuel, tools, shelter, boats—and medicines, such as quinine and sarsaparilla. The rainforest provides rubber, gums, balsams, and chocolate. Its plants also are the source of curare for poisoned darts, although local hunters also use the venom from poison-dart frogs. These are strikingly brightly colored frogs that secrete powerful toxins from glands on their backs and whose color announces their deadly aspect to predators. Potentially lethal frogs include the golden poison-dart frog *(Phyllobates terribilis)* that lives close to Colombia's Pacific coast and is one of the most poisonous creatures on this planet—one milligram of its toxin is powerful enough to kill between 10 and 20 humans.

*Above:* This epiphytic aroid is thriving on a rainforest tree trunk. Aroids are extraordinarily diverse plants with attractive foliage. They can serve as a source of medicinal substances.

*Right:* The yellow-banded poison-dart frog lives in rainforests in Venezuela, northern Brazil, and Colombia, usually in humid conditions among trees, rocks, or leaf litter. Its beautiful vibrantly 'painted' skin is highly toxic.

## At Home in the Forest

Between 2500 and 3000 species of fish inhabit the Amazon and its countless tributaries and they supplement their diet in these nutrient-poor waters with fruits, nuts, and leaves that fall into the water. There are many tetras and piranhas, dogtooth fish (with huge canine-like teeth) which grow to 3ft (1m) in length, as well as hatchetfish that can take short flights out of the water, propelled by their large winglike pectoral fins, if alarmed by a predator or when catching small flying insects.

The Amazon basin is home to the increasingly rare giant otters that are often found in noisy playful groups. Sloths seem to drip from the trees as they progress slowly upside-down along the branches far above a forest floor pinpricked with gleaming beetles. In the trees are squawking parrots, brilliant hyacinth and scarlet macaws, hummingbirds seeking succulent nectar, and about 40 different species of toucans with huge bright bills that are used to peel the skin from fruit. The cartoon-like hoatzin bird flaunts its red eyes and blue facial skin below a spray of rakish feathers. Sharing the arboreal canopy are some 36 monkey species including golden lion tamarins, squirrel monkeys, howler monkeys, woolly monkeys with their gentle eyes and deep-pile fur, and the large woolly spider monkeys that live in the Atlantic forests of southeastern Brazil.

Brilliant gleaming boa constrictors and emerald tree boas loop through the trees in search of prey. The great hairy tarantulas found here are the largest spiders on earth and include some bird-catching varieties, such as the goliath birdeater which has a legspan of up to 12in (30cm) across. Army ants march along forest trails in aggressive foraging groups, while leafcutter ants (one of the most widespread Amazon rainforest insects) build gigantic anthill-homes for their three million or so residents. They hope to avoid the attentions of the giant armadillo *(Priodontes maximus)* that feeds primarily on ants and can rapidly consume the entire population of a termite mound. These powerful animals have strong claws with which they dig for food and make burrows.

**Above:** Squirrel monkeys live together in groups of up to 500 individuals in the tropical forests of Central and South America.

**Left:** The red oscar cichlid lives in warm slow-moving water, often sheltering under submerged branches in the Amazon river basin. They have dark orange-ringed spots, or ocelli, on their dorsal fins that may perhaps serve to deter piranhas from nipping their fins.

**Opposite:** The superb hyacinth macaw is the world's largest flying parrot at 39in (100cm) long with a 48–56in (120–140cm) wingspan. It has beautiful blue plumage that extends over all the body except for some black under the wings.

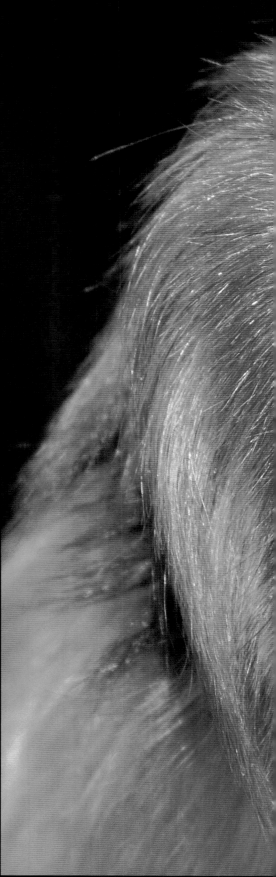

**Above:** *Rare giant otters live as a cohesive group, collaborating to protect their large 'campsite' territories and their young. They have dense fur, webbed feet, and a powerful tail to propel them through freshwater rivers, streams, lakes, and springs as they hunt fish.*

**Right:** *The golden lion tamarin lives in Brazil's coastal jungles and is one of the globe's most endangered—and most exotic-looking—monkeys, with a mane of long amber hair and golden eyes. Generally, one breeding pair will control a group of about a dozen individuals.*

## When Evening Falls

Eventually the sun sets behind the forest and a myriad pink and golden shades flush the darkening sky as stealthy jaguars emerge to hunt deer, tapirs, wild pigs, or smaller mammals and reptiles. At sunset, the beautifully patterned ocelot *(Leopardus pardalis)* may also appear. This small 3ft (1m) long wild cat hunts in many forests in Latin America but is becoming increasingly rare. Since ancient Aztec times, its fur has been highly prized and now, with deforestation of its habitat an added threat, this beautiful cat's survival is threatened.

There are about 950 different species of bats to be found in the Amazon including the world's only true vampire bat that arrives, silent and stealthy, to pierce the flesh of sleeping mammals (often domesticated animals such as horses, cattle, pigs, and goats) with its razor-sharp teeth and lap up the blood on which it feeds. Vampire bats tend to live in colonies—ranging in number from a few individuals to thousands—in dark caves, hollow trees, and old buildings.

Safe from prying eyes in the gathering dark, dwarf porcupines make their secretive forays along river banks in search of food while, in the silvery-bubbled water, yellow and olive-green anacondas swim along smoothly, their nostrils atop their snouts so that they can breathe easily in the water. Caimans are types of alligator with eyes that glow red in torch-light. They drift past hunting for prey that includes fish, amphibians, reptiles, and water birds. As darkness falls and the jungle reverberates to the echoing calls of its nocturnal inhabitants, meteor showers often sparkle across deep velvet starry skies and the hazy band of the Milky Way stretches high above the forest canopy.

*Background: The sun sets crimson and gold over the broad flow of the Amazon River as night life stirs in the forests on its flanks. Bats flit from their perches, unfurling folded wings that have been wrapped around them as they slept in dark caves. Now they prepare to hunt in the hours of darkness, ready to swoop unerringly upon their prey.*

# Plateaus, Plains, and Pampas

The word 'plain' can mean simple, even boring perhaps, but the plains of Latin America are anything but dull! They are full of fascinating life forms and steeped in history. There are vast fertile stretches of prairie in the so-called 'bread-basket' of Argentina as well as huge plateaus and high flatlands (often used for grazing and farming), while yet more grassy plains undulate below startling azure skies in Brazil and Venezuela.

Narrow coastal plains wriggle along the Gulf of Mexico and the Atlantic coastline of northeastern South America and down much of South America's Pacific coastline. Mexico's Gulf coastal plain extends for 900 miles (1450km) from Tamaulipas state (on the Texas border) to the Yucatán peninsula and includes the Tabasco Plain in its southeastern section—a hot humid zone with heavy rainfall which is overlaid with dense, tropical forest while its triangular northern portion is dotted with lagoons.

*Above:* In northern Argentina vast pampas meadows—spotted with tussocks of grass and the promise of marshland in wetter times of the year—stretch away into the distance under cloud-tossed skies.

*Left:* In Bolivia's Altiplano the Andes are at their widest and incorporate between their peaks one of the globe's most extensive areas of high plateau, second only to Tibet. This is a cool, semiarid, windswept place.

## Remains of Ancient Civilizations

Notable historic attractions include the pre-Columbian Olmec ruins of La Venta and the Mayan brick-built ruins of Comalcalco. Farther north and west, the densely populated Mexican Plateau is set between the Sierra Madre Oriental and Sierra Madre Occidental mountains.

The people of Venezuela and Colombia have been raising cattle for hundreds of years on vast fertile grassland plains called llanos, which track along the Caribbean coast of South America and occupy some 220,000sq miles (570,000km²). In the colonial period, the cowboys here (called llaneros) herded millions of cattle and, indeed, cattle breeding remains the most important economic activity.

## The Altiplano

Nestled among the mountains in the central Andes region of South America and covering parts of Peru, Bolivia, Chile, and Argentina is the Altiplano—which means 'high plain.' Except for Tibet, this is the globe's most extensive area of high plateau lying at about 12,000ft (3650m) above sea level. Strong winds sweep across it every day, becoming more intense after noon, and often it resembles a semidesert with whirling dust devils that skim across the land. In the Pleistocene epoch, around a million years ago, there was an enormous lake here, of which some evidence remains today in the form of Lakes Titicaca and Poopó. They may seem vast to our eyes but they are mere puddles in comparison to their prehistoric source.

The Altiplano plains are home to steppe-type plants including tough shrubs, cactus scrub, and patches of meadow-like vegetation, surrounded by mountains and volcanic cones. In addition, there are immense stretches of sparkling white salt deposits, hot springs, and the occasional tiny rustic village typically with its colonial church. Among the tussocks of grass and high steppes live foxes and camel-like beasts—llama, vicuña, guanaco, and alpaca—while the clear blue and emerald lakes are home to abundant bird life, such as black and white geese, flamingos, crested ducks, and Andean avocets. Common rhea *(Rhea americana)*, an ostrich-like bird that stands about 4ft (1.2m) tall, run quickly over the flat plain on their long, powerful legs and three-toed feet, while condors soar on thermals above this remote wilderness.

*Right: Lake Chungará is one of the world's highest lakes, set beside snow-capped Parinacota volcano in northern Chile. Aymará shepherds reside here in clay and straw village buildings. They graze vicuña and grow alfalfa. The Altiplano forms a flat terrace within the high Andes at an average altitude of 13,100ft (4000m). Volcanic peaks rise yet higher.*

## Mato Grosso

Spreading over much of central Brazil and across the southwest to Bolivia and Peru, is the Mato Grosso plateau, a sparsely populated area of forests and grasslands that are part of the Brazilian Highlands, essentially an enormous plain rippled by a handful of smallish mountain ranges. The principal activities here are cattle-raising and mining. Another important and nationally protected area of Brazil, the beautiful uplifted plateau of the Chapada dos Guimarães is blessed with savannah, red rock cliffs, ancient cave paintings, canyons, and waterfalls that include the 260ft (79m) Véu da Noiva cascade in Itatiaia National Park—an impressive torrent often visited by brilliant red macaws. This tableland area marks the transition between the campo cerrado plateau area and the Amazon rainforest.

*Below: Long-legged maned wolves stalk the Brazilian savannah.*

*Opposite: The mountains and craggy cliffs of Chapada dos Guimarães in central Brazil are surrounded by high plains known as cerrado.*

## Brazilian Cerrado

Beautifully spotted jaguars slink through the scrubby tundra of the high plains of the Brazilian cerrado, in the 1.2 million sq miles (3 million km²) of Brazil's central plateau which has the highest level of plant diversity of any of the globe's savannahs—some 10,000 species, 44 percent of which are unique, as well as 300 or so mammal species and 935 species of birds. The campo cerrado is home to pumas, marsh and pampas deer, giant anteaters, and the shy maned wolf *(Chrysocyon brachyurus)*. Named for its erectile black mane, this is the largest of South America's dog family, with reddish golden fur like a fox and very long black legs that have earned it the nickname of 'stilt-legged fox.' They help it to be able to keep a lookout for prey above the tall savannah grasses. Often the wolves defecate on the nests of leafcutter ants and the insects then use this dung to fertilize the fungus gardens which provide them with food. Only a few thousand maned wolves remain in the wild and habitat loss caused by agricultural expansion remains a threat to their survival.

# Patagonia

Patagonia (a geographical region which lies in southern Argentina) has low flatlands, often tiered in terraces to create a vast steppe region. Up to 280 species of endemic plants survive on the vast windswept volcanic plateaus. Among the world's most sparsely populated regions, this remote area offers a refuge to the guanaco, Darwin's rhea, and the Patagonian mara *(Dolichotis patagonum)*, a rodent which looks rather like a small deer with its long slender legs and large ears. It lives on the plains and scrubland, sometimes making low grumbles or whistling calls to its young. Another rodent, the highly sociable degu, is found only in Chile. It lives in burrows, digging communally to construct large underground living quarters.

There are armadillos here too, including the giant armadillo *(Priodontes maximus)*, which is well protected in a bony shell that acts like a suit of armor to deter predators. They use their sharp claws to dig for food like grubs and to make their dens or underground burrows. The name armadillo means 'little armored creature' and it was coined by the Spanish conquistadores, while the Aztec name was azotochtli, which means 'tortoise-rabbit.'

Rather smaller is the mouse opossum *(Marmosa murina)*, a solitary nocturnal marsupial that has dispensed with the usual pouch to protect its young: the babies simply cling onto a teat until old enough to ride on their mother's back, tenaciously gripping her fur. These little creatures often inhabit forested regions as well as the grassy plains.

The greater grison *(Galictis vittata)* is a type of ferret that lives in both woodlands and grasslands in Central and South America, emerging from crevices in rocky areas and beneath tree roots to feed on rodents, which it kills with a swift bite to the back of the neck.

Peccaries are common throughout Central and South America and bear a close resemblance to pigs. Like pigs, these medium-sized mammals have a snout ending in a disk of cartilage and eyes that are small relative to the size of their head. Peccaries are omnivorous, with a preferred diet of roots, grass, seeds, and fruit although they will also eat small animals. The jaws and short, straight tusks of peccaries are adapted for crushing hard seeds and slicing into plant roots. They also use their sharp tusks to defend themselves from predators.

*Left: Set in Argentina and Chile and named by Magellan, Patagonia was once believed to be the home of giants who towered 5m (over 16ft) in height. In fact, the native tribes here averaged only 1.80m (6ft) tall but most 16th-century Spanish invaders were a mere 1.5m (5ft) or so.*

*Left:* The vast Los Glaciares National Park in Patagonia is a UNESCO World Heritage Site. In its mountains, lakes, and forests many creatures live including cougars, guanacos, foxes, deer, and ducks. Over 1000 bird species are found here, with eagles and condors often seen soaring above the lofty peaks.

***Top left:*** The Patagonian mara is a large guinea pig-like rodent that pops out of its burrows to graze. Pairs mate for life, rearing their young pups in a communal crèche burrow.

***Above left:*** As summer retreats in Patagonia, the leaves flash bronze and crimson against a turquoise lake, heralding the approach of cold winter and the promise of snow.

***Top right:*** The Patagonian landscape blazes with pink flowers and golden grasses. Tussock-grasses and shrubs seem to crouch close to moorland and boggy terrain below blue skies.

***Above right:*** An armadillo pauses to sniff the air before trotting off again—surprisingly quickly. If threatened, it will roll up into an armor-plated ball or flee into the scrub.

# Pampas Lands

In Argentina and Uruguay, the grassy treeless plains are known as pampas—after a Quechua Indian word meaning 'flat surface.' Here welcome spring rainfall and fertile soils help the local people to produce grain and to raise both grazing sheep and the renowned strains of Argentinian cattle. Maize, cassava (manioc), and other crops are cultivated here. Humid pampas stretch along the seaboard while dry pampas can be found in the west and south, but, despite their respective descriptions, this terrain also alters with the season. However wet and soggy it is in spring, it will be baked dry and subject to frequent fires once summer arrives.

Pampas lands are home to many unique creatures such as giant anteaters and coypu (Myocastor coypus), large semi-aquatic rodents that look like huge guinea pigs. They are 16–24in (40–60cm) long, with an additional 12–18in (30–45cm) of tail, and live in waterside burrows. The plains viscacha (Lagostomus maximus) has distinctive black facial markings that give it the appearance of sporting a mustache. It is the largest member of the chinchilla family and resembles a large guinea pig. It lives in a system of underground burrows in the barren areas of the high pampas. Unusual birds found in the pampas regions include rheas and ovenbirds, such as the rufous hornero (Furnarius rufus). They are named for their domed mud nests which resemble the shape of a Dutch oven.

Long before the Spanish arrived, the pampas region was inhabited by hunters (who netted fleet-footed guanacos and rheas) and fishermen, followed later by sparse populations of nomadic foragers. By 1536 the Spanish conquistadores under Pedro de Mendoza had arrived. They founded Buenos Aires and made their homes in Argentina. This is now the world's eighth largest country, covering an area of 1.1 million sq miles (2.8 million km²).

From the mid-18th to the mid-19th century, the Argentine and Uruguayan grasslands were famous for the rough-riding gauchos, nomadic horsemen and cowhands (often of mixed European and Indian ancestory) who became folk heroes, enshrined in romantic tales just as their Wild West counterparts became part of North American folklore. These hard-working and often itinerant horsemen caught wild horses, tamed them and used them to round up cattle that (like the horses) had escaped from the early Spanish settlements. Scattered throughout the region are many historic estancias, fine ranches that today often offer visitors guided trail rides, polo lessons and a chance to ride along with the gauchos or admire their world-class horsemanship as they break in a young horse.

*Below:* The pampas of Latin America are where gauchos first honed their skills on Spanish ranches (estancias) set in the rolling grasslands.

## Grass Panoramas

The seemingly endless pampas of Argentina cover around 300,000sq miles (777,000km²)—almost 25 percent of the nation. At a glance, the landscape appears level but, in fact, from near sea level in the east it rises gently toward the west. Where once, long ago, trees may have flourished, today the flat or softly rolling pampas are covered with grasses, including many stipa species, often called feather, needle, or spear grass. Pampas grass (*Cortaderia selloana*) is a large perennial grass native to Brazil, Argentina, and Chile. Its huge clumps can soar up 10ft (3m), bearing tall silvery-white or pinkish silken plumes. It was introduced into North America and Europe as an ornamental grass for gardens. The grasslands are dotted with a mosaic of lakes, ponds, and wetlands.

*Background:* The term pampas derives from Native American Quechua words denoting a flat treeless area where only tall grasses grow to relieve this monotony. In late summer pampas grass has delicate silken plumes, which can rise high above its sharp-edged blue-green or silver-gray leaves.

# Life on the Pampas

Crab-eating foxes *(Cerdocyon thous)* sometimes haunt grassy areas as well as forested zones, their gray-brown coats frequently tinged with yellow. Whether solitary or in pairs, they spend their days in burrows, emerging at night to find fruit or hunt for small prey, insects, and turtles—especially in the llanos, the flat plains and tropical grasslands east of the Andes in Venezuela and Colombia. During the wet season, these foxes seek out crabs on the muddy floodplains to eat in their dens.

The Patagonian fox or (common) Andean fox is the second largest native canid in Latin America after the maned wolf. It has gray and reddish fur, a white chin, reddish legs, and a stripe on its back that may be barely visible. It inhabits open pampas and deciduous forests and feeds on rodents, rabbits, birds, lizards, and carrion.

There are pampas cats *(Leopardus pajeros)* in both Argentina and Chile as well as the more widespread Geoffroy's cat *(Leopardus geoffroyi)*. They are supremely well camouflaged when hunting in the grassland's dense ground cover for small birds, lizards, insects, and rodents.

The pampas provides habitats for many birds too, ranging from tiny flycatchers and hummingbirds that measure only 3in (8cm) long to common rheas *(Rhea americana)* that stand almost as tall as a human. They are one of the largest Latin American birds at 60lb (27kg) in weight and measure some 4ft (1.2m) in height. They are challenged in size only by the condors that soar high above the Andes—these are the largest birds capable of flying with an amazing wingspan that can reach 11ft (3.3m) and a length of about 4ft (1.2m).

Beneath the condors roll seemingly endless grassy plains, sometimes dotted with marshes and wetlands that glint in the ever-changing light. The sun glows on sweeping golden, ocher and green-tinged landscapes, as the clouds scud along, creating dancing shadows below them as they race across vast open skies.

*Right:* The Patagonian fox or culpeo may be seen in open country in the western Andes, where it hunts rabbits, rodents, lizards, and birds.

*Below:* Geoffroy's cat is, with the puma, the most southerly wild cat in the world. This agile climber often sleeps among tree branches.

# Swamps and Wetlands

Vast marshes flow in green swathes through many parts of Latin America but the greatest of these is the Pantanal, a floodplain in Brazil formed where the Paraguay River extends into the border areas of southeastern Bolivia and northeastern Paraguay. It claims the title of being the world's largest swamp, with the majority of its wetlands lying in the Brazilian states of Mato Grosso and Mato Grosso do Sul. Subject to flooding in December, the river reaches its highest watermark in June at which point it turns into an immense swamp, submerging over 80 percent of the area and flooding some 54,000sq miles (140,000km²)—an area larger than Greece.

*Above:* The floodplain wetland system of the Pantanal is home to an impressive diversity of spectacular wildlife. Birds include great white egrets which develop superb plumage during the breeding season and spread out their elegant snow-white feathers during courtship displays. Here one is seen alighting on the Paraguay River.

*Left:* The giant water lily (Victoria amazonica)—the first bloom of the day opens as early morning casts its magic glow over the Pantanal. Discovered by explorers in 1801, specimens were collected and cultivated in Europe. By the mid-19th century, the giant water lily was a much-prized exhibit in many European botanical gardens.

## The Pantanal

The Pantanal encompasses a variety of ecological subregions within its large river areas, standing water, marshes, and lakes—all manner of wetlands, in fact—and often it represents a halfway transition between aquatic and terrestrial worlds. Few roads penetrate its watery midst and so this vital ecosystem is a veritable Garden of Eden for wildlife, providing a much-needed home for many endangered or threatened species.

An estimated 1650 species of plants, over 650 species of birds, 260 species of fish, around 120 species of mammals, and 130 species of reptiles and amphibians flourish here. Lurking in the waters, always on the lookout for fish on which to feed, are about 10 million Yacare caimans (*Caiman yacare*), possibly the highest concentration of crocodilians in the world. These caimans are prized for their skins and so are especially threatened by trapping. Sadly, in the 1970s and 1980s, some 1 million skins were illegally poached each year.

*Opposite:* A symbol of the Pantanal, the jabiru stork is the tallest flying Latin American bird—some males stand about 5ft (1.5m) high. It has superb snowy plumage but a featherless black head and upper neck.

*Right:* The wetlands at Pousada Piuval provide excellent habitats for birds, caimans, and piranhas. The annual Pantanal flooding creates vast lagoons full of fish and mollusks, upon which many other creatures feed.

*Below:* The Pantanal is the world's largest wetland area, and teems with wildlife, including caimans. These powerful reptiles eat fish, as well as preying on birds, turtles, and land-dwelling animals like capybara and deer.

This wetland is a haven for three giants—giant armadillos, giant anteaters, and giant otters—as well as cougars, jaguars, iguanas, maned wolves, monkeys, marsh deer, and ocelots. The world's largest living rodents, capybaras, are estimated to approach a population of 500,000 in the Brazilian Pantanal.

The Pantanal is a natural home to 26 species of parrot, including the magnificent hyacinth macaw (*Anodorhynchus hyacinthinus*), the globe's largest parrot species that may reach a length of over 3ft (1m). It is named for its glorious blue plumage; it also has bright yellow lines around its eyes and on its beak. The bird is well advised to seek refuge in this remote region as illegally captured specimens can command a US$10,000 price tag on the black market.

A less likely candidate for poachers is the Brazilian or lowland tapir (*Tapirus terrestris*) which has a long, rubbery nose that forms a small trunk. This shy hoofed mammal spends a good deal of time cooling off in water or wet mud and is an unexpectedly good swimmer.

Standing up to 5ft (1.5m) tall and seen in large groups close to rivers and ponds, the jabiru stork (*Jabiru mycteria*) is the tallest flying bird found in Latin America. It consumes prodigious quantities of fish, mollusks and any other tasty morsels that its long beak can snatch. Although it is an ungainly bird on the ground, the jabiru is a powerful and graceful flier. The 650 or so species of bird here also include blue and yellow macaws, red and green macaws (or green-wing macaws), blue-fronted parrots, herons, egrets, storks, spoonbills, ibises, ducks, kingfishers, toco toucans, and snail kites that earn their name from their habit of swooping down to feed on large snails.

## Gran Chaco Swamps

Argentina has swamp areas in Gran Chaco that, during the rainy season, also are transformed from hot arid regions as the rivers flood in, swiftly turning dry land into marsh. Upstream, along Argentina's River Plate, many endless-seeming swamps stretch out to the horizon decked with floating ferns and water lilies. At the Paraná delta where the Paraná and Uruguay Rivers meet and flow into the River Plate, the local people raise water buffalo on the fertile plains, while the nearby wetlands and streams are inhabited by water turtles, alligators, otters, and swamp deer.

## Brilliant Waters

The Iberá wetlands lie in the center of Corrientes province in northeast Argentina and provide the second greatest wetland of South America, where over 350 different species of birds can be seen. In the Guaraní Indian language the word iberá means 'brilliant waters.' Some 3500sq miles (9000km²) was flooded almost 10,000 years ago by the Paraná River although certain parts of Iberá are covered by sand dunes, relics of an ancient period of drought before the swamps were formed by a dramatic climatic change. The swamps and lakes of Iberá are fed by rainwater—some 79in (200cm) of rain falls each year which drains away very slowly.

This vast sweep of wetland is very humid and almost uninhabited by humans but is amazingly full of wildlife. It is home to 380 different kinds of birds including birds of prey, such as owls and hawks, as well as American storks, plumbeous ibises, and countless species of ducks. Other wading birds stalk the waters in search of food, including jabiru storks, spoonbills, herons, flamingos, ibises, and anhingas (snakebirds).

There are marshes, mangrove swamps, and wetlands in Central America too, with Panama being noted for its swamps and the attendant swarms of mosquitoes that flourish in the high humidity. Other creatures found in these marshy regions include pink-flushed Chilean flamingos and Coscoroba swans (the smallest of all the swan species) that eat grasses, small water plants, mussels, and fish that populate the well-vegetated swamps and lagoons. Frogs abound in these watery wonderlands and the smoky frog is common along the banks of the natural network of scenic and navigable waterways in Costa Rica's Tortuguero National Park. The glass frog also lives here. It is an amazing reptile whose internal organs are visible through its transparent skin.

*Right: Living by lagoons, the marsh deer is Latin America's largest deer.*

*Below: Emerald tussocks fringe a swamp lake in Mendoza, Argentina.*

## Amazon's Swamps and Marshes

Marshes are also found amid tropical forests in the Amazon basin where flooded swamp forests represent some 3.9 percent of the Amazon biome. In northeastern Brazil, palm swamps are regularly inundated and the plants survive under water for most of the time. The Jaraná palm, in particular, can survive virtual 'drowning' for some eight months each year.

At just over 15,500sq miles (40,000km²), Marajó Island in the Amazon delta is the largest fluvial island in the world, i.e. one created from sediment deposited by the river. During the rainy season around half of the island is flooded and turns into swamp, bustling with hundreds of bird species including egrets, flamingos, herons, parrots, ducks, hawks, toucans, and graceful scarlet ibises with their long curved beaks. Water buffaloes wallow in the swampy terrain, sharing the watery habitat with (among others) alligators, capybaras, and great anacondas.

## Palm and Mangrove Swamps

Colombia's palm swamps flank the mighty Orinoco River where seasonally flooded plains lead into a delta of swamp forests and coastal mangroves. Here the endemic but increasingly rare Orinoco crocodile grows to a staggering 23ft (7m) in length. Other endangered species in this region include the Orinoco turtle, giant armadillo, giant otter, and black-and-chestnut eagle.

Swamp forests thrive in the hot zones close to Ecuador where ocean salt water meets fresh river water. In the Ucayali River in Peru the swamps are dominated by Mauritia palms, their fallen fronds gradually decomposing in the perpetual standing blackwater. Parrots and macaws swoop and call around the forest canopy. Here are found hummingbirds, ocher-bellied flycatchers, and point-tailed palmcreepers which have rich chestnut plumage and sharp silver bills that can probe the crevices of palm crowns and dead hanging fronds. Their calls are ringing rattles while white-bearded manakins crackle and trill in the branches. Blue-and-gold macaws (Ara ararauna), one of the biggest parrots in the world, nest in the deep hollow trunks of dead palms.

Mangroves in the Manglares de Tumbes National Sanctuary in Peru include the red, black, and white varieties as well as the button mangrove. This is a perfect habitat for snails, crustaceans, mollusks, and more than 100 fish species that sometimes succumb to the hungry jaws of the now-rare American crocodile (Crocodylus acutus) or the crab-eating raccoon (Procyon cancrivorus). Magnificent frigatebirds soar on the warm updrafts while sharp-billed herons stalk the shallow water in search of prey.

These wetlands provide the perfect habitat for bullfrogs, horned frogs and tree frogs and, as dusk falls, bats leave their daytime roosts to flit silently over the tangled roots and dark water as they hunt for insects. These swamps are at their lushest between April and November; from December to March much of these wetlands dries out.

**Below:** *Bactris palms fringe an Amazonian oxbow lake. The bactris fruit provides a seasonal feast for toucans and macaws in the nearby jungle.*

*Piranhas may also enjoy a windfall as they devour many different fruits when the land is flooded and they can swim among the tree trunks.*

*Left: A tangle of palms is steeped in rippling water. The Amazon boasts over half of the globe's remaining rainforests and is its largest and most species-rich area of tropical trees, waterways, and wildlife.*

***Top:*** *The muddy orange waters of a flooded rainforest swamp. Brazil has the world's greatest area of undisturbed frontier forest, measuring some 772,300sq miles (2,000,000km²).*

***Above:*** *Mangrove swamps grow along almost all of the Brazilian coast, a precious link between sea and land, rich with organic deposits derived from leaves, animal droppings, mineral salts, and tidal residue.*

# Arid Deserts

The Chihuahuan Desert, straddling the Mexican/US border, is the world's most biologically diverse desert. It seems able to withstand the recent invasion of creosote shrubs which have elbowed aside many native plants. Here too flourishes the mesquite, an extremely hardy, drought-tolerant plant which draws water through a long taproot that may grow some 190ft (58m) deep into the earth. Dry rocky slopes support agave plants which grow in the form of thick fleshy leaf rosettes. For centuries the locals have used agave to make all sorts of items including pens, nails, needles, nets, string, weaving thread, and to produce the spirit tequila. This is most often derived from distilling the sap of the blue variety *(Agave tequilana azul)*, especially around the town called Tequila in the highlands of western Mexico.

*Above:* A beautiful blue-green agave plant that grows in the Mexican desert. It has rosettes of thick rigid leaves often edged with marginal spikes and some have an extremely sharp terminal spine. Many agaves produce musky odors to attract the bats that pollinate them, while others emit sweet perfumes to lure insects.

*Left:* Under an azure sky huge petrified tree stumps are scattered over the desert. These are remnants of the mighty forests which covered Patagonia 150 million years ago, during Jurassic times. They were preserved by the volcanic ash of massive Cretaceous eruptions and now form a haunting testament to constantly shifting landscapes.

## Prickly Pears

The spiny prickly pear (or Indian fig) is a type of cactus that thrives in dry zones stretching from Mexico to southern Argentina. They can range from a squat 12in (30cm) in height to an imposing 7ft (2m). The most common species used in cooking is the Indian fig opuntia (*O. ficus-indica*): their fruits are edible, as are the cactus pads that are cooked as a vegetable once the sharp spines have been removed. The pulp of prickly pear is said to lower unhealthy cholesterol levels in the blood and the fruit's pectin reduces the need for insulin in diabetics, while the soluble fibers of both fruits and pads help to stabilize blood sugar levels. The flowers may appear as yellow, red, or purple blooms, even on plants of the same species, and they are pollinated by bees that collect the nectar to feed to their developing larvae.

Desert woodrats or packrats use prickly pear cacti both as a home and as a source of food, building nests which provide protection from coyotes (animals that in Mexico are thought to have diabolical power, especially if they cross your path). Woodrat nests may be raided by rattlesnakes, which not only kill and eat the small rodents but also take over their residence. Various birds also use the cacti for nests and roosting sites while many land animals like blacktailed jackrabbits, rock iguanas, and collared peccaries eat the ripe fruit and fleshy pads—as do giant cactus beetles and cactus weevils.

## Crimson Treasure

Also found feeding on the cacti is the tiny cochineal beetle that is the source of a brilliant red or purple dye; its rich coloring was used to dye royal garments long before people discovered its more mundane contemporary use as a food coloring. The Aztecs valued red dye higher even than gold and scoured the desert for female cochineal beetles—it takes about 155,000 of these little insects to make 2.2lb (1kg) of extract. Spanish conquistadores soon discovered the secret and cochineal beetles joined Peruvian gold as valuable cargo in the galleons that sailed across the seas to Europe. The Spanish traded the dried beetles to make a brilliant crimson dye for fabrics and illuminating documents. In the early 15th century, the artist Michelangelo used it as a pigment with which to paint and, more recently, the first US flag had cochineal-colored red stripes.

*Opposite:* Cactus varieties in Mexico include the spiky agave, the flower-tipped candelabra with its multiple branches that resemble the tentacles of a huge sea anenome stranded far from the ocean, and the upright thrust of giant cardon cactus.

*Below:* A prickly pear cactus bristles in the Sonoran desert near the Mexican border. Despite its sharp spines, this cactus may be home to many creatures, from snakes to jackrabbits, nesting birds, and the tiny cochineal beetles from which precious crimson dye is extracted.

## A Very Grand Canyon

Chihuahua's Copper Canyon—a 23,000sq mile (59,570km²) network featuring six distinct canyons—was formed over millennia by the erosion of its rivers. It outdoes even the United States Grand Canyon both in terms of scale and because of its searing temperatures. Since ancient times this area has been the home of the Tarahumara Indian tribe, descendants of the ancient Aztecs, but today their fragile existence is threatened by prolonged heatwaves and severe drought. The Copper Canyon railroad runs from Los Mochis near the Pacific coast to Chihuahua City and is a stunning engineering achievement that opened in 1961. Over 400 miles (650km) in length, it encompasses 39 bridges—one stretches over 1640ft (500m)—and 86 tunnels, with the longest over 4900ft (1500m) as it courses through rugged terrain, hugging steep mountainsides and crossing deep ravines.

# The Sonoran Desert

The Sonoran (or Gila) Desert also straddles the Mexican/U border. This is a vast and very hot desert, occupying an area of 120,000sq miles (311,000km²). Defying desert stereotypes the Sonoran Desert is one of the globe's wettest, in some places irrigated by up to 15in (39cm) of annual rain which generally falls during the monsoon season. The desert is home to some 60 species of mammal, 350 birds, 20 amphibians over 100 reptiles, 30 native fish, and more than 2000 native plant species. Its vegetation is the most diverse of the North American deserts. Its unique flora and fauna include the saguaro *(Carnegiea gigantea)*, a large, tree-sized, candelabra shaped cactus that can take up to 75 years to develop jus one side arm. This desert is the only place where it grows i the wild. Its night-blooming flowers, which only appear afte about 50 years, are usually pollinated by bats (primarily lesse long-nosed bats) that feed on the nectar of its flowers.

Not so long ago, many gray wolves roamed central Mexicc but numbers subsequently declined and the Mexican wolf wa listed as an endangered species in 1976. Sadly, it has now vanished from the region. Fortunately, before their demise, several were caught in Chihuahua and have survived and successfully bred in the Arizona-Sonora Desert Museum. By 1998, 11 wolves had been released back into the deserts of Arizona.

Birds, such as the gilded flicker, build their nest holes in the majestic saguaros, their excavations sometimes penetrating the cactus ribs and damaging or killing the plant. Gila woodpecker create new nest holes in them each season, rather than reuse the old ones, thus leaving conveniently empty nests that attrac a variety of other creatures, such as the elf owl *(Micrathen whitneyi)*, the world's second smallest owl at a mere 5–12ir (12–30cm) in height. Elf owls pursue flying insects for food and also eat scorpions, deftly managing to nip off the stinger to avoid being stung.

**Opposite above:** *It was its deep orange color that gave Mexico's steep-walled Copper Canyon (Barrancas del Cobre) its name. The canyon is the focus of a national park in a remote and awe-inspiring location.*

**Above:** *The deeply ribbed branches of this ancient saguaro cactus frame the rising moon. These tree-sized giants may live for 200 years and are pollinated by bats, which relish the nectar of their night-blooming flowers*

**Left:** *This is desolate terrain in the very aptly named Mushroom Valley near Creel, Copper Canyon, an area that boasts many amazing rock formations including one called Elephant Rock. There are also stunning waterfalls and gushing hot springs in the area*

# The Atacama Desert

While the Sonoran Desert receives at least some rainfall, Chile's Atacama Desert is the globe's driest place. Some regions here have seen no rainfall since records began—some parts may have been dry for 400 years. Running from the Pacific Ocean to the Andes Mountains, with an average width of less than 100 miles (160km), much of the desert extends high up into the Andes mountains and is actually a relatively cool place, with daily temperatures ranging between 32°F and 77°F (0°C to 25°C) according to the season.

Set at one end of the Atacama is Bolivia's vast Salar de Uyuni—the world's largest salt flat—which measures 4085sq miles (10,582km²) in area. Vast deposits of saline crystals glitter on its smooth white surface. Flocks of Chilean flamingos (*Phoenicopterus chilensis*) live in and around the salt lakes feeding on the red algae that bloom in the waters. Regardless of how little it rains, there is always a reserve of underground water here as the El Tatio geysers prove. These consist of over 80 small but vigorous water spurts and columns of steam, which are best viewed at dawn as the vapor soon evaporates once the air warms.

NASA tests its lunar and Mars exploration vehicles on the moon-like surface of the Atacama Desert, a sharp contrast to the traditional cultures that have flourished here where reminders of an ancient past include human and animal figures carved on barren hillsides. Somehow, more than a million people survive in this parched land, living mainly on its fringes in coastal cities and villages. Astronomers are attracted to the region because they can take advantage of the clear dry atmosphere to probe the skies with their telescopes. The desert is a famous source of Chile saltpeter (sodium nitrate), which is used in the production of explosives. This is the only place in the world where, free from rainfall dissolution, it has accumulated in enormous quantities.

In this hyperarid world, just a few hardy creatures survive, living on the moisture derived from fog and dew, in an environment where the hum of flies and insects typical of forest habitats is markedly absent. In this bone-dry climate, the bodies of buried Indians have been preserved, turning into mummies in the parched ground. Some of the world's oldest mummies (at 9000 years old) have been found in the Atacama Desert.

*Right: Numerous geysers spurt plumes of steam at El Tatio in the Atacama Desert and make a remarkably spectacular display early in the morning when their outpouring of scalding hot water offers a sharp contrast to the cold ambient temperatures here, some 13,800ft (4200m) high in the Andes.*

**Left:** The Arbol de Piedra (Rock Tree) at Uyuni, in Bolivia, is just one of many fascinating contorted rock formations to be found here, often towering impossibly high and endowed with bulbous swellings. They are best seen in the early morning when their strange shapes reflect the rosy glow of the dawn sunlight.

**Background:** Crystals shimmer on the mirror-like surface of Salar de Uyuni, the world's largest salt flat, set in Bolivia's high plateau region. Countless flamingos may be seen here, and the flocks are at their most numerous in September, striding across the blanched remains of a prehistoric inland sea.

# The Sechura Desert

The Sechura (or Peruvian) Desert runs north from the Atacama along the northwestern South American coast, mainly along Peru's western coast, and also fringing Chile. It is crossed by numerous short rivers, many of which trickle into oblivion, exhausted before they can reach the ocean. This is a region of deep canyons, migrating dunes, and sparse scrublands, home to cuis cerrano, a relative of the guinea pig, that establish their foraging paths between tussocks of riverside grasses. Once the ancient Moche peoples' diet included guinea pigs that are native to the Andes and which were originally domesticated to provide a ready source of food. Archaeological digs in Peru and Ecuador have unearthed artifacts depicting guinea pigs dating from AD 100 to AD 500, indicating that the Moche worshiped the animals as well as eating them. As the moon rises, the Sechuran fox *(Pseudalopex sechurae)* that has spent its daylight hours sleeping in an underground den emerges to hunt for beetles, rodents, birds, carrion, seed pods, or small armadillos that have also emerged from their burrows.

*Above:* Massive petrified trees litter the barren flats of the central Patagonia Desert in what is one of the globe's best preserved petrified forests. Many trees were already 1000 years old when they were killed by prehistoric volcanic eruptions and buried in the ashes.

*Opposite left:* The desert near Ica in Peru has enormous dunes that are among the world's richest hunting grounds for marine fossils. Here lie the remains of hundreds of ancient whale forms and megalodon sharks.

*Opposite right:* Ancient cave paintings in Patagonia where people have lived and hunted for thousands of years. The cave images include depictions of guanacos that still roam the Patagonian plains.

# The Patagonia Desert

Indigenous tribes once executed cave paintings in Argentina's windy Patagonia Desert, set in the shadow of the Andes in the southern portion of the Argentinian mainland. This is the Americas' largest desert and the world's fifth biggest, occupying 260,000sq miles (673,000km²), with its central zone home to an amazingly well-preserved petrified forest. Aquatic grasses and larger plants cling to its fringes and around ephemeral lakes. The steppe-like plains are, however, generally treeless. The desert supports a surprising variety of creatures including burrowing owls, lesser rheas, foxes, weasels, pumas, pygmy armadillos, desert iguanas, and venomous sand spiders.

## Harsh Environments

The Monte is a warm shrub desert in Argentina, set north of the Patagonia Desert and east of the Andes. Shrubs, grasses, and tall cacti rise in its more hospitable areas while herbaceous species, including wild irises and lilies, may appear after the summer rain. The animal life is similar to that of the Patagonia Desert but with even greater diversity, boasting many small mammals like mice as well as guanacos, tuco-tucos (gopher-like rodents), boa constrictors, and lizards.

La Guajira Desert, in northernmost Colombia (in fact, the northernmost point of South America) covers most of the La Guajira peninsula, which juts into the Caribbean Sea. This is a region of hot arid plains, cactus, and desert scrub. It also holds considerable coal reserves. Farther south, Colombia's Tatacoa Desert is famed for its fossil remains and is home to several endemic species of spiders, snakes, scorpions, lizards, and eagles that thrive in its tropical desert climate.

## Snakes, Scorpions, and Lizards

No image of the Mexican desert would be complete without its famous rattlesnakes (*Crotalus* and *Sistrurus* species). Mexico and Central America are home to four subspecies while South America has nine in total. The snake warns off intruders using the distinctive sizzling castanet of its rattle but, if approached, it may then strike rapidly, drawing its body into an S-shaped coil and lunging forward. Its venom, an enzyme/protein complex, is one of the most dangerous natural animal poisons, which not only immobilizes and kills the prey but also initiates the process of digestion. Most rattlesnakes are nocturnal, hiding away during the heat of the day and emerging at twilight to hunt for prey.

Other poisonous desert creatures include lancehead vipers, highly venomous fer-de-lance snakes, and scorpions—there are some 1300 scorpion species worldwide and they are thought to have existed for about 425–450 million years. They have been found at elevations of over 12,000ft (3660m) in the Andes Mountains as well as in coastal dunes and deserts. Scorpions are nocturnal and ambush their prey, lying in wait and then seizing and killing insects, spiders, centipedes, other scorpions, lizards, snakes, and mice. They are able to regulate the delivery of their venom in proportion to the size of the target that they have selected.

*Right: The western diamondback rattlesnake hunts small birds or mammals by night and in the early morning but can survive long periods without food. Here its forked tongue 'tastes' the air. Aggressive and with powerful venom, it is responsible for most of the snakebite fatalities in northern Mexico.*

Various whiptail lizards and tegu lizards are distributed throughout the West Indies and South America. They emerge from shady cover or burrows to bask in the sun. Whiptails prefer relatively high body temperatures and once their bodies are warm enough they scurry off to forage for insect larvae,

ants, or termites that they dig out of the leaf litter. In the skies above the desert, vultures and eagles soar on invisible pockets of warm rising air, scanning the landscape for any movement in the arid world far below them which might indicate an opportunity to feed.

# Conservation Areas and Parks

Today, many of the world's most precious natural habitats are threatened and, in an effort to preserve these wild remote areas, Latin American nations are striving to establish conservation zones and national parks to protect wildlife, especially the most vulnerable endangered species.

These parks include Chile's 700sq miles (1810km²) Torres del Paine National Park that encompasses scrubland set beside glistening rivers and lakes, low forest, tundra, pasturelands, and high altitude forests. As well as providing excellent habitats for pumas, guanacos, foxes, and skunks, the park is home to numerous birds including Andean condors, black-chested buzzard eagles, black-necked swans, Chilean flamingos, spectacled ducks, woodpeckers, and kingfishers.

*Above: Guanacos always seem to turn their heads to face the same direction, perhaps trying to detect sound or movement. They inhabit arid mountainous regions and run quickly through steep rocky terrain. This pair is roaming through Chile's Torres del Paine National Park.*

*Left: Dramatic rock formations rear toward the sky as clouds are driven along by unrelenting Patagonian winds. This is Torres del Paine National Park, the name derived from its spectacular granite towers (torres in Spanish). Glaciers and snow-capped peaks feed mighty waterfalls that plummet down sheer cliffs into thick forests far below.*

## Special Conservation Areas

In 2002 the government of Brazil announced the creation of the largest tropical forest reserve in the world—the Tumucumaque National Park in Amapá bordering French Guiana and Suriname. At 15,000sq miles (38,700km²) it is about the size of Switzerland. This vast and largely unexplored region of Amazon forest contains rushing rivers and waterfalls, with massive granite outcrops looming above pristine forest and giant trees. It contains species, particularly fish and aquatic birds, found nowhere else on Earth.

Ecuador's Galápagos Islands National Park encompasses 19 major and minor islands as well as 42 islets. The reserve protects over 2700sq miles (6937km²) of land and around 51,350sq miles (133,000km²) of the Pacific Ocean. Often referred to as a naturalist's dream, these very special islands provide scientists and tourists alike with the opportunity to observe (among other creatures) giant tortoises, marine iguanas, blue-footed boobies, dolphins, sharks, and manta rays.

Cotopaxi National Park, in Ecuador, a few hours' drive away from the capital Quito, boasts one of the highest active volcanoes in the world—also called Cotopaxi—which peaks at 19,347ft (5897m), offering amazing scenery and views from the rim of the crater. As well as a wide variety of indigenous wildlife there are herds of wild horses in the park, whose ancestors escaped from the care of the earliest Spaniards who introduced them to the American continent. Limpiopungo Lake is a popular tourist destination in the park and a nesting site for Andean gulls. Andean condors may also sometimes be seen here, soaring high on the warm thermal currents.

Manu National Park and Biosphere Reserve in Peru protects almost the entire watershed of the River Manu and also extends up the slopes of the Andes. It includes some of the globe's most important habitats—Andean grasslands, elfin forests, cloud forests, and lowland Amazon rainforests. The many protected creatures that live here include 800 bird, 200 mammal, 100 bat, plus 120 fish and reptile species. Giant otters, black caimans, giant armadillos, capybaras, jaguars, spectacled bears, tapirs, ocelots, and many primates thrive in these wild and spectacular environments.

*Opposite: The Galápagos giant tortoise is the world's largest living tortoise, with a life expectancy in the wild estimated to be more than 150 years. It has become one of the most symbolic animals of the Galápagos Islands.*

*Below: Mount Cotopaxi in Ecuador is one of the world's highest active volcanoes and the highlight of this national park in the Andean Highlands.*

## Many Natural Splendors

The 520sq mile (1350km²) Pantanal National Park (see also page 98) is located in one of the world's most immense, biologically diverse environments and is part of the largest freshwater wetland system on the planet, stretching through southwest Brazil and parts of Bolivia and Paraguay. It provides breeding sites for enormous numbers of wildfowl. A wide variety of flora and fauna are found in the park, including large populations of jaguars, capybaras, marsh deer, giant anteaters, tapirs, and hyacinth macaws.

Iguaçu National Park (see also page 39) lies at the meeting point of Brazil, Argentina, and Paraguay where the Iguaçu River tumbles down to the Paraná river in 275 splendid waterfalls—higher than Niagara Falls and wider than Victoria Falls. The Iguaçu's banks are densely populated by trees, including the ceibo or cockspur coral tree, whose bloom is Argentina's national flower. Both parks are home to a wide variety of wildlife including several endangered species—jaguars, jaguarundi, tapirs, ocelots, jungle eagles, and Yacare caimans.

Bolivia's Kaa-Iya National Park in the Great American Chaco region offers some of South America's greatest natural splendors with a wide variety of habitats that range from arid savannah, cerrado (woodland savannah), gallery forest, and thorn scrub to dry tropical forest. Despite the park's arid climate it is a refuge for jaguars and pumas and home to some 100 species of mammals. This is the only national park in Latin America for which a Native American organization shares administrative responsibilities with the national government.

With 26 national parks, 58 wildlife refuges, 32 protected zones, and several special conservation areas and reserves, Costa Rica has set aside some 25 percent of its country's land to safeguard many beautiful and incredibly biodiverse environments from deforestation and logging. Costa Rica is often referred to as 'the living Eden' and this tiny country is home to an astonishing 10,000 species of plants and trees, more than 850 species of birds, 200 species of mammals, 220 species of reptiles, and some 35,000 species of insects. Some of Costa Rica's most popular parks include: the Arenal Volcano National Park—which contains the country's most active volcano; the Barra Honda National Park—with pre-Columbian limestone caves; the Corcovado National Park—one of the most biologically diverse places on Earth and the Las Baulas National Marine Park—annual nesting site for about 800 female leatherback turtles.

There are many more such wonderful parks and reserves in Latin America, some of them covering huge areas and containing great terrain diversity—from Mexico's 67 national parks in the north to Tierra del Fuego National Park. This provides a final dramatic flourish at the southern tip of the Andes with spectacular valleys, forests, rivers, glacial lakes, gorges, and a magnificent coastline above which albatrosses soar.

*Background: Argentina's equivalent to the United States Grand Canyon is the amazing Sierra de las Quijadas National Park. Dramatic red sandstone formations rise where, many millennia ago, pterosaurs ruled the skies. Countless fossils and prehistoric footprints remain here today.*

**Left:** *Bolivia has pristine, wild, and rugged national parks, encompassing biologically diverse regions that support a surprising variety of wildlife. Here birds gather on the blanched white shore of a shallow lagoon. The landscape appears empty but, in fact, many life forms thrive in this habitat.*

**Top:** *Iguaçu National Park, famous for its magnificent waterfalls, is also home to howler monkeys, jaguars, ocelots, tapirs, and anteaters.*

**Above:** *Dramatic caves have been carved out of this Monte León cliff in Patagonia, an area of rugged offshore rocks and jagged stacks.*

# Deforestation and Climate Change

The Amazonian jungles are truly immense—with countless trees towering above dense verdant understory, through which serpentine rivers thread their way. Lush vegetation drips with moisture in this humid environment, creating a hothouse that supports a greater variety of exotic wildlife than any other of the globe's habitats.

Sadly, today this important ecosystem is seriously threatened. Brazil boasts 56 percent of the Amazon forests but the highest deforestation rates are actually in Ecuador, which is feeling the effects caused by the demands of an increasing population, and in Argentina, where expanding agricultural frontiers continue to encroach on forested land. A recent report claims that just over 70 percent of greenhouse gas emissions in Latin America come from Brazil, Mexico, Venezuela, and Argentina. It is therefore vital to 'pull out all the stops' to limit the worst effects of invasive forestry, vanishing habitats, and, in particular, to protect the vital role of Amazonia in preserving the world's climate stability.

Deforestation—and the climate change that follows in its wake—has attracted much media attention recently so that greater efforts are being made to spearhead and support conservation movements and nature reserves. Global warming (caused by greenhouse gases in the atmosphere that are mainly produced by the burning of fossil fuels) has a worldwide impact that is becoming all too apparent. It has already led to the growing intensity and frequency of the hurricane season in the Caribbean, changes in rainfall patterns, increased water levels in rivers in Argentina and Brazil, and the shrinking of glaciers in the extreme southern regions of Patagonia and the Andes range.

This precious reserve of energy and life is also the Earth's major oxygenator. One fifth of the world's fresh water flows along the Amazon River. Fed by pounding rainfall, the massive network of waterways and tributaries streams past forests described as the 'lungs of our planet' as the trees continuously convert carbon dioxide into oxygen in the course of their cycle of respiration, producing over 20 percent of the world's supply. These trees and plants take carbon dioxide from the atmosphere and store it in roots, stems, leaves, and branches. Rainforests also recycle water—the Amazon forest alone pumps more than 20 billion tons of fresh water into the atmosphere every day.

The survival of many of these wonderful forests and their wildlife is threatened by the logging industry, fires, the expansion of agriculture, and growing centers of population that encroach hungrily on the environment. The soil of a tropical rainforest is a fragile layer, deposited over many centuries but only a mere 3–4in (7–10cm) thick. This vulnerable veneer is a vital resource that protects the precious humus and the spreading roots of the giant trees that arch above. About 99 percent of nutrients are held in root mats while the spread of the forest canopy above acts as a buffer, softening the torrential rainfall into a gentle sprinkle that falls on the earth below. When a portion of rainforest is destroyed, the full force of the beating rain washes away the precious humus and the thin soil soon degrades and loses its fertility. As the land bakes to a hard, cracked clay mosaic under the burning heat of the sun, a swirling dust bowl soon develops. The soil here is likely to be whirled away by winds or becomes susceptible to flooding in the next tropical downpour.

# The Future

Despite the threats outlined above, there is still reason to be optimistic about the astoundingly complex and varied world that is Latin America. There are powerful measures in force now as many conservation movements and organizations address the problems and seek solutions to protect some of the richest and most exciting habitats on Earth. Even after the incalculable loss of about 58 percent of Brazil's frontier forests, over 772,200sq miles (2,000,000km²) remain—constituting some 30 to 40 percent of the globe's remaining tropical rainforest. This is home to over 56,000 listed plant species, as well as 1700 bird, 695 amphibian, 578 mammal, and 651 reptile species. These jungles are an amazing source of medicines too. The compounds derived from forest plants include curare (used as an anesthetic and to relax muscles during surgery), quinine obtained from chinchona bark that serves to treat and prevent malaria and substances from some 2000 varieties of tropical plants that are potential cures for cancer and other diseases.

A multitude of marvelous and precious creatures flourish on land and in the oceans, rivers, and lakes that wash the shores and weave through the landscape. Each and every one is a vital element in the amazing patchwork quilt of dramatic and colorful landscapes that is Latin America.

*Opposite:* Silver waterfalls tumble through the greenery of pristine Amazon rainforests. Myriad creatures flourish here, as they do throughout Latin America—in sea, lake, and waterway; on dazzling desert sands and islands; beside steaming volcanoes or in shimmering pampas plains. They thrive amid the ooze of swamps and wetlands, scramble up sheer mountains, or soar in blue skies above this marvelous continent.

The nations of Latin America encompass an extraordinary amalgam of cultures and heritage, a vibrant blend that combines the influences of original civilizations with the Portuguese and Spanish lifestyle that arrived in the wake of Columbus from 1492. As the name for the leaders of Spanish expeditions in the 16th century—conquistadores—suggests, the Spanish conquered, seized, and ruled, supplanting or overwhelming the local culture and imposing their own, spreading through vast territories as they did so.

*Left and above:* Latin America is home to many nations and traditions; a tapestry of cultures whose colorful threads weave an extravaganza of festivals, carnivals, bright costumes, music and dance, sacred places, art, and sculpture.

# PEOPLE AND CULTURE

# A New World

The very first Americans probably arrived some 12,000 years ago, traveling from Asia into Alaska across a land bridge that then existed across the Bering Strait. Gradually people spread to all parts of the North and South American continents and in time these indigenous tribes developed into a series of important civilizations, including the Aztecs, Toltecs, Maya, and Incas.

Once the Europeans arrived in the late 15th and 16th centuries, life in Latin America changed forever. The indigenous rulers and elite societies, such as the Incas and Aztecs, ultimately lost power but they did retain many traditions and beliefs, hoping for an ultimate return to the status quo. Spain and Portugal busily established more and more colonies, which in due course were split according to the principles established by Pope Alexander VI's 1493 Line of Demarcation—whereby Spain claimed all the areas to the west and Portugal took the eastern section that would subsequently become Brazil.

*Above:* An Inca mask, its simply decorated gold surface still gleaming. Incas regarded gold as 'the sweat of the sun' believing it reflected the glory of their sun god. Many fine artifacts were plundered by the conquistadores but, hidden away, some escaped this pillage.

*Left:* Machu Picchu's ancient stone buildings flow down the steeply terraced mountainside in Peru. Hidden in the Urubamba Valley jungle in the Sacred Valley of the Incas, the immaculate stonework is linked by some 3000 steps. More than half of the buildings served a religious purpose.

## Missionary Zeal

European culture and the Roman Catholic faith spread quickly throughout the continent, with frequent intermarriage between indigenous people and the colonists speeding up this process. Soon *mestizos* (those of mixed European and Amerindian ancestry) dominated the population in several colonies. Throughout the succeeding centuries, the impact of Europeans on Latin America was immense.

The European colonists were equipped with considerable missionary zeal and they raised countless Hispanic missions for the growing numbers of converts to the Christian faith. Many Latin American landscapes today are punctuated by early Hispanic churches whose tall bell towers rise impressively into the azure skies. In 1533, Holy Roman Emperor Charles V despatched the first Franciscan monks to the Americas. Soon missions had been established and by the mid-17th century the Jesuit order (which had been founded in 1534 by Ignatius de Loyola with a specific missionary purpose) was a veritable colonial power in its own right with missions in Argentina, Brazil, Bolivia, Mexico, Uruguay, and Paraguay, all enjoying a good measure of independence from Spain and Portugal. Today visitors can tour the grandiose ruins and magnificent churches which were once the centers of Roman Catholic religion and education for indigenous populations.

**Above:** *The simple elegance of a Hispanic mission, once a vital religious outpost, is outlined by the deep blue Mexican sky behind its fine curves.*

**Opposite:** *An old colonial Catholic church in Argentina, bleached white and dusted with red desert sand—a lonely outpost with enormous impact.*

Many small villages with little more than a church and plaza soon developed into thriving towns as houses, colleges, hospitals, workshops, and warehouses sprang up. Eventually, Spanish and Portuguese rulers feared that the Jesuits were becoming too powerful and influential and, as a result, many missions were attacked and the Jesuits were expelled from South America in 1767.

As well as Catholicism, the conquistadores brought less welcome cargo in the form of guns, slaves, and European diseases like smallpox, measles, whooping cough, tuberculosis, chicken pox, typhoid fever, scarlet fever, diphtheria, mumps, and influenza. These illnesses may have been responsible for the deaths of more than 20 percent of the local population. Increased trade and the widespread transportation of goods— often infiltrated by rats, fleas, and other disease carriers— meant that some epidemics reached local communities before even a single European had set foot in the area.

## Foreign Exchange

By way of a more favorable exchange, the Hispanics took back to their homelands all sorts of valuable commodities including cotton, chocolate, tobacco, potatoes, sugar, and useful medications such as quinine. They also transferred crops within the region, taking coconuts to the Bahamas and coffee to Brazil. New timbers, such as mahogany, arrived in Europe from the West Indies while trade in sugar (which replaced honey as a sweetening agent), tobacco, and slavery had a huge impact on the Caribbean way of life.

The Spanish style of cattle ranching was imported to the Americas by the conquistadores. When Francisco Vasquez Coronado explored what is now New Mexico and Arizona in the 1540s, he took with him cattle and horses, some of which escaped to the wild and bred, ultimately spreading all over the grassland prairies. Cattle drives started in Mexico in the mid-16th century, and then spread to other regions as vaqueros (which means 'cowboy' in Spanish) tended and moved herds of cattle.

By the late 19th century one out of every three cowboys was a Mexican vaquero, working as cattle drivers for a ranch or a mission. These brilliant horsemen were often of mixed race (mestizos or mulattos—people of mixed European and African descent). As a consequence, despite their skills, they had low social status. In the early settling of California—when it was still owned by Mexico—the term buckaroo was used for these fine herdsmen while they were variously called gaucho in Argentina, llanero in Venezuela and Colombia, and huaso in Chile.

**Top:** *Argentinian gauchos ride in traditional dress. As well as their role in cattle ranching, gauchos are now an important element in the tourist trade, with many estancias offering accommodation for horse-riding enthusiasts.*

**Above:** *This gaucho's costume includes a finely decorated knife clipped to a woven sash.*

**Background:** *Gauchos' skilled horsemanship is still an essential part of herding cattle.*

# Amazing Civilizations

Long before the Spanish and Portuguese arrived, Latin America was peopled by many splendid civilizations. Their ways of life and death, their beliefs and their rituals (such as human sacrifice) profoundly influenced their art and architecture and many surviving temples and palaces reflect this rich heritage.

Some of the first temple complexes were built on the Andean coastline as early as 2600 BC when the Mayan culture was founded in the Yucatán peninsula. Soon pyramids and ceremonial centers were being built in Mexico and Peru while the Classic period of Mayan civilization peaked in about AD 250 in present-day southern Mexico, western Honduras, El Salvador, northern Belize, and Guatemala (with its great ancient city of El Mirador).

Many fine civilizations evolved over the years: the Moche flourished in north Peru between AD 100 and 800; at around the same date the Nazca created their renowned carving of vast intricate lines and patterns in the south Peru desert; and in Mexico's huge city of Teotihuacan, the Pyramids of the Sun and Moon were built as vast populations gathered in the largest city in the Americas in pre-Aztec times. Later, through the 6th and 7th centuries AD, Teotihuacan evolved into a vital trading center with as many as 600 pyramids being constructed in what was then the world's sixth largest city.

Other great cities included Tiahuanaco in Bolivia, the Zapotec capital at Monte Albán in southern Mexico, and the Yucatán's amazing Chichén Itzá which in 900 was the center of Mayan culture.

Over the centuries, the Zapotec and fierce Toltecs, who controlled much of central Mexico, established powerful civilizations, which eventually waned. The 12th century witnessed the height of Chimú civilization in Peru but soon the power of the Incas, initially a farming community, rose as their warrior chiefs developed the city of Cuzco in the southeast of the country. Their empire grew and, through the 15th century, spread right through the central Andes, despite wars with the Chimú. The Incas' eighth ruler, Viracocha, was a major empire builder. The Incas were the largest pre-Columbian state in the New World. Mexico's Aztec empire also expanded dramatically as two marshy islands in Lake Texcoco became the focus of Tenochtitlán—a great metropolis that would later become Mexico City.

**Left:** *A temple at Tikal, Guatemala, the largest ancient Mayan city to have been discovered and now a UNESCO World Heritage Site with magnificent monumental architecture set amid lowland rainforest.*

**Opposite:** *The House of Turtles and a pyramid at Uxmal, a vast Yucatán city, once home to some 25,000 Maya. It flourished in the Late Classic period (AD 600–900). Human sacrifices took place at the Pyramid of the Magician temple.*

**Below:** *Ek' Balam in Yucatán is an impressive Mayan city. The site contains temples and pyramids as well as a splendid central plaza bordered by three massive ceremonial structures.*

## Inca and Aztec Strongholds

As the Aztec empire linked the cities of Tenochtitlán, Texcoco, and Tlacopan, the Inca empire dominated the central Andes and reached as far as Ecuador in the north. A great fortress was raised in Cuzco in the 1440s, forming the heart of the empire, while the amazing city of Machu Picchu was built about 1450. The Incas were a most advanced culture, governing some 12 million subjects and communicating efficiently, despite having no written language. Runners carried messages through the 11,000 mile (18,000km) road network, up and down sheer mountainsides and over rope bridges swinging above deep ravines to meet four main highways that entered Cuzco. Inca historians kept detailed accounting records through an encoding system of color-coded, knotted strings to represent numbers called quipu—sometimes referred to as 'talking knots.'

During the mid-15th century, while the Incas set about conquering the Chimú and extending their empire into Bolivia, Chile, and Argentina and as far as Peru's southern coast, the magnificent Aztec ruler Montezuma I conquered vast areas of Mexico and had a huge temple built in Tenochtitlán. This city absorbed Tlatelolco as the empire reached its height. In 1487, no less than 20,000 captives of war were sacrificed at its great temple pyramid.

*Above:* Peruvian girls in traditional dress, their costumes a flurry of color against the massive stones used to construct Machu Picchu's walls. Beyond steep precipices, several Inca rope and tree-trunk bridges provided vital links to this elusive site.

*Left:* Machu Picchu boasts one of the most dramatic settings of any of the world's famous archaeological sites. Its remote location deep in the jungle and high in the mountains meant that it escaped Spanish plunder and was virtually unknown to Europeans until its 'rediscovery' in 1911.

The fruit of the cacao tree was being consumed in the form of a drink by the Olmecs thousands of years before the Aztec civilization was established. The Mayans further developed the spicy, bittersweet drink by roasting and pounding raw cacao beans with maize and capsicum peppers and letting the mixture ferment. The tree was widely worshiped and the Aztecs credited their feathered serpent god, Quetzalcóatl, with introducing the cacao bean to their land even though they were unable to cultivate it in the high Andes. They procured the precious beans either through trade or military conquest. Chocolate was the preserve of nobility and warriors (whose virility was said to be improved by its consumption) while the beans also served as currency—tribute and taxes were paid in cacao beans to the Aztec emperors—30 beans could buy a small rabbit and 100 could purchase a slave.

The great Aztec ruler Montezuma II and his court consumed up to 50 pitchers of xocolatl (chocolate) a day. In 1519, Montezuma, convinced that Spanish explorer Hernán Cortés represented the white bearded god whose coming was prophesied, introduced him to xocolatl, served in a golden goblet—and presented him with a royal plantation of cacao trees. In fact, Montezuma valued xocolatl more than gold and after his defeat and death, when the victorious conquistadores searched his palace and treasury, all that they found were vast quantities of cacao beans.

## Inca Gold

The Incas made wonderful silver and gold ornaments, including full-size replicas of cobs of maize. Gold ore, nuggets, and flakes extracted from mountain rivers were smelted with charcoal, using bellows to heat the furnace, in order to liquefy and so collect the precious metal—a craft derived from Chimú artisans. The Incas did not use gold as currency; it served purely for adornment or ceremonial purposes—as vessels, jewelry, figurines, or to decorate tombs and temples, with gold representing 'the sweat of the sun' and silver 'the tears of the moon.'

Hard labor served as currency, with tributes paid in the physical energy required to build temples, fortresses, agricultural terraces, and roads. However, more gold arrived as tribute or gifts from chiefs and governors under Inca rule. By the time the Spaniards invaded Peru, Cuzco was the New World's richest city. The last Inca ruler, Atahualpa, who was captured by Francisco Pizarro in 1532, offered his captor for his release enough gold and silver to fill his prison cell as high as Pizarro could stretch up with his hand. Pizarro accepted

was brutally executed by garrote. Soon, the fine temples and palaces were looted, the artistic beauty of gold artifacts was ignored as the treasures were melted down to make ingots, enabling easier transport. Amazingly, the wealth generated by this seized Inca gold was sufficient to transform the entire European economy as it became the prime source of gold.

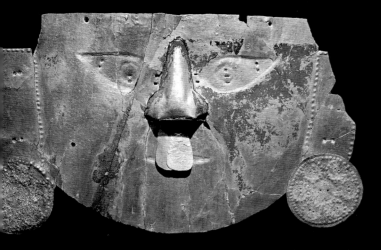

*Left and below:* A simple Inca gold mask and a more extravagantly decorated example. Gold was used not only for revered objects and decoration but also for everyday items—carpentry nails, eating utensils, eyebrow tweezers, and combs. The rich hauls that Spanish conquistadores acquired as they looted this amazing wealth—in a region where chocolate was sometimes prized more highly than gold—was a huge catalyst for change in European economies.

# Encountering the Explorers

The history of the exploration of Latin America includes the stories of many courageous adventurers who set sail across uncharted waters, supposedly full of dragons and monsters, and marched on determinedly through unmapped lands in search of treasure and adventure. This era of exploration was exemplified by Italian Christopher Columbus, the first European officially to discover the New World. He sailed from Spain across the Atlantic Ocean in 1492, hoping to find a route to India but landed in the Bahamas and then Hispaniola in the Caribbean instead.

Italian explorer Amerigo Vespucci was the first person to realize that the Americas were separate from Asia after his voyage of 1501–02. America was named for him in 1507, when a German mapmaker first used the name America for the New World. In 1499–1500, Vespucci had been the navigator for Alonso de Ojeda when they discovered the mouth of the Amazon and Orinoco Rivers in South America. On his second expedition to the continent he mapped portions of South America's eastern coast.

*Above and left:* An old engraving and present-day replicas of Christopher Columbus' ships sailing into uncharted waters. Ultimately, after a perilous sea voyage during which he overcame the crew's terror and a potential mutiny, Columbus would discover the New World.

## Braving Uncharted Seas

Spaniard Hernán Cortés sailed with 11 ships from Cuba to the Yucatán Peninsula to look for gold and silver and to secure the interior of Mexico for colonization. In 1519 he conquered the Aztecs, having uncompromisingly burned his fleet so that his army was committed to succeed by conquest or die. With the help of local rebels, they overthrew the ruler and chief priest, Montezuma II, and seized the Aztec Empire, replacing bloodthirsty Aztec rituals with Christianity. Using brutal force, they established Spanish government and seized large quantities of gold and silver in the process.

Meanwhile, Francisco Pizarro set about eliminating the Incan rule in western South America. He had initially accompanied Ojeda to Colombia in 1510 and was with Vasco Núñez de Balboa when he crossed the Panama isthmus to become the first European to gaze upon the eastern Pacific Ocean in 1513. Hearing of the fabled wealth of the Incas, Pizarro explored Peru's Pacific coast and then crossed the mighty Andes with a mere 175 or so men. He seized the Inca capital Cuzco, conquered the Inca empire, and founded the present-day capital city of Lima.

Other renowned explorers and discoverers include the Portuguese Bartolomeu Dias who sailed off the coast of South America on an expedition in 1500 and spotted land at Espírito Santo in Brazil. Ferdinand Magellan was the renowned Portuguese explorer who led the first expedition that sailed around the globe in 1519–22 although he was killed in the Philippines in the course of the voyage. It was he who named the Pacific Ocean—perhaps having seen it in one of its more peaceful moods—and he is recognized as the first explorer to enter the Pacific from the Strait of Magellan and to reach Tierra del Fuego. Vincente Yáñez Pinzón, a Spanish explorer and navigator who had commanded one of the ships on Columbus' expedition of 1492, sailed to the Brazilian coast and in 1499 explored the Amazon rivermouth and then sailed north to northeastern Venezuela.

Moving inland, Francisco Hernández de Córdoba, a Spanish slave trader, explored Mexico in 1517 and Nicaragua in 1524, while Pedro de Alvarado conquered El Salvador and the Guatemala highlands. Spaniard Álvar Núñez Cabeza de Vaca made an amazing journey in 1528, walking from Tampa Bay, Florida, to Mexico City, a trek that took some eight years and during which most of his party died. He also explored South America's Paraguay River. Somewhat later, it was Juan Bautista de Anza, a Mexican-born explorer, who in 1774–76 established an overland trail from Mexico to the northern Pacific coast of California and found a possible corridor through the desolate Sonoran Desert.

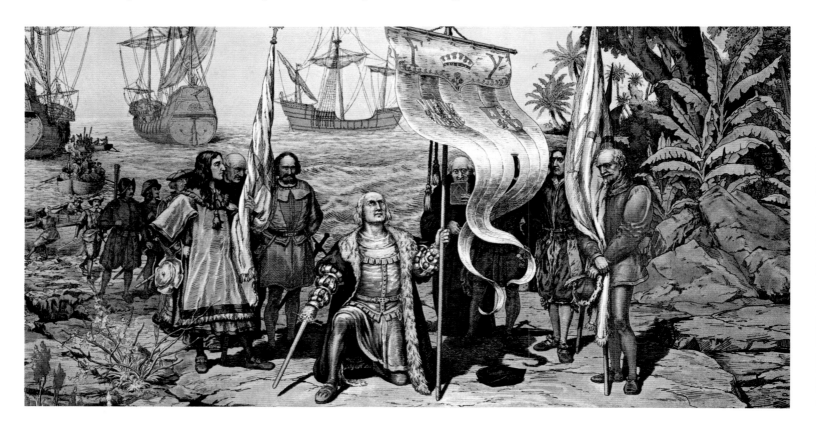

**Above:** *Columbus makes his 1492 landfall on San Salvador in today's Bahamas, an event now celebrated as Columbus Day (October 12).*

**Opposite:** *Hernán Cortés arrives in Mexico; the locals are unaware of their future exploitation and the conquests that will bring them war and disease.*

# Latin America's Original Inhabitants

In the first days of this wave of exploration, in just one generation, some 300,000 Spaniards and Portuguese emigrated to the New World, infiltrating, infecting, dominating, driving away, and sometimes ousting altogether the indigenous ethnic groups. Some survived this onslaught—especially in the most remote locations amid dense jungle where pockets of the original tribes remained undisturbed. Today, however, even these most isolated groups are subject to contact by the outside world and the inevitable change this brings.

In the Gulf of Mexico and the Caribbean Sea, islands such as Puerto Rico, Hispaniola, and Cuba were inhabited from the second millennium BC by hunter-gatherers. In due course, Neolithic American-Indian farmers, the Arawak, gradually moved north through the island chain and, from about AD 1000, fierce Caribs expanded their territory through ruthless warfare, often absorbing their enemies literally—by eating them—and then marrying the women. When Columbus met the friendly Arawak—whom he described as Indians because he initially believed he had reached India—he conferred on these locals this inaccurate name, just as the region was called the West Indies. In 1492, there were five Taíno kingdoms and territories on Hispaniola (today's Dominican Republic and Haiti), each led by a tribute-taking chieftain. The Taíno were an Arawak subgroup.

Meanwhile, the warlike Caribs were raiding Puerto Rico's coast. The Spaniards were fascinated by these man-eating cannibals (whom Arawak called canibas) who ferociously resisted interference, wielding clubs and shooting poisoned arrows at anyone who disturbed them. They dyed their bodies red, inspiring the notion of a red-skinned race, and sailed to remote places, fishing with their hands or nets and sometimes using powerful herbs to anesthetize the catch.

As well as the Incas and Aztecs (see pages 138–143) the indigenous peoples of the region included seminomadic tribes, hunter-gathers, fishermen, and migrant farmers. Coastal zones and riverbanks teemed with hundreds of thousands of people enjoying a veritable paradise in this undisturbed world, bursting with wildlife and flora. In Brazil, an estimated 2000 different nations and tribes existed at one time but most vanished in the wake of European settlement. Some survived, of course, albeit often as slaves, miners, or laborers, but only those who lived in remote less-charted territories retained their ancient culture.

*Below and opposite: When the first explorers landed, coast and riverside villages bustled with indigenous peoples who came down to investigate the approaching vessels. The contrast between the Europeans and the native Latin American residents must have surprised both the newcomers and the people they now confronted.*

# The People of Latin America

The term Latin America was coined during Napoleon III's campaign to install Maximilian I as Emperor of Mexico in 1864 but, in fact, the region encompasses people who speak a range of languages, including German in Paraguay and Welsh in Patagonia. Spanish and Portuguese tongues do dominate, however, for despite the diverse ancestries of Latin American immigrants, when these newcomers arrived, they soon integrated and most of their descendants spoke only Spanish or, in Brazil, Portuguese. People of Italian descent make up half of Argentina's and Uruguay's populations but only a few actually speak Italian.

The notable exception to this is southern Brazil where some German and Italian communities have retained their native languages. Outside Italy, Brazil has the largest population of Italians, with the city of São Paulo boasting more Italian residents than Rome—while Mexico has the world's largest Spanish-speaking population.

*Above:* A woman from Lake Titicaca where a small population of people live on Uros—artificial floating islands which are made of reeds.

*Left:* The bright traditional clothes of Peru include wonderful woven shawls, warm woolen garments, ponchos, bright multilayered petticoats, and skirts—often featuring traditional tapestry work and embroidery.

## A Mixed Population

The racial and ethnic mix varies across the nations and some native languages do survive, like Quechua in Peru plus Mixtec and Kekchi, while the Carib language evolved into modern Creole, carrying with it a few traces of its original vocabulary. Creole mathematical skills involved counting up to five, with ten characterized by 'all my fingers' and 20 indicated as the digits on both hands and feet. More than 20 was referred to as being the same as the hairs on their heads!

Today's Latin American population is an amalgam of different heritages and ethnic groups and includes many people of African and Asian descent, with the slave trade having contributed significantly to the mix. There were at least 50 million indigenous people when the Europeans arrived in 1492, concentrated in the highlands of central and southern Mexico and in South America's Andean region. Now, despite the virtual decimation of indigenous societies, the total population of Latin America has risen to some 560,000,000 and includes an amazing 192,000,000 living in Brazil, around one-third of the region's population.

*Right:* Kuna people are a tribal society who are found on the San Blas Archipelago, Panama. They depend on agriculture for their subsistence.

*Below right:* In Salvador de Bahia, Brazil, the ancestry of many local people can be traced back to the days of black African slavery.

*Below:* In the late 15th century large numbers of European colonists settled in South America and most white Latin Americans are of Spanish or Portuguese origin.

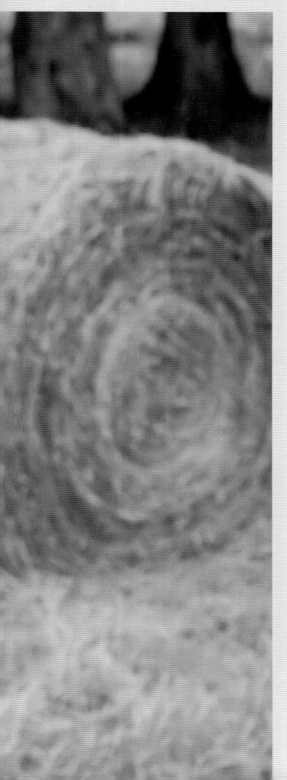

## Religion

As the Spanish invaded their new territories, they introduced their own militant brand of Catholicism (a dogma that back home, from 1478, would culminate in the Spanish Inquisition to stamp out heresy and question the faith of the many new converts from the Jewish faith). Zealous missionaries supplanted many sun-worshiping cults but, while local communities submitted to their new rulers, the ancient beliefs still resonated for many of the indigenous population.

Sun worship, especially in the pre-Columbian societie of Mexico and Peru, involved complex ceremonies that we enacted at massive stepped flat-topped temples. The Azte bred dogs, eagles, jaguars, and deer specifically for sacrifice well as despatching butterflies and hummingbirds to hon the god Quetzalcóatl. Human victims were escorted to the t of the temple, laid on a stone slab by priests, and then ritua sliced open. One priest would tear out the still-beating he and place this in a bowl held by a god statue, as the body v

*Below:* Chichén Itzá in Mexico was an important Mayan religious center, with fine temples and magnificent carvings depicting their gods. It was the site of human sacrifice on a vast scale; hundreds of victims had their hearts cut out on temple altars by priests who then cast the bodies down steep blood-drenched steps.

thrown upon the temple stairs. It was believed that this blood-letting provided nourishment for the Sun. Other bloodthirsty rituals included gladiators battling to death, arrow shooting, flayings, or burnings to honor the fire god.

## Spirit Worship

The Caribs worshiped ancestor spirits, in particular the good or evil maboya. Sickness, defeat in battle, or even death might result from an enemy maboya's spell. Led by traditional healers and priests, they believed in immortality of the soul and, as their bodies were buried and possessions burned, any of their slaves who failed to escape were killed too.

Today, while several of the world's major religions are practiced here, most Latin Americans are Christians with the Roman Catholic faith being dominant. Indigenous beliefs are still maintained in several places, however, with various Afro-American faiths upheld and tribal voodoo still being present in Cuba and Brazil.

*Background:* Silhouette of the giant statue of Christ the Redeemer with his outstretched arms above the city of Rio de Janeiro, a symbol of both the Holy Cross and all-embracing Christianity. Some 74 percent of Brazilians (about 142 million) are said to be of Roman Catholic faith.

*Below:* The ornate interior of Santa Clara church (Querétaro, Mexico), is a Baroque masterpiece, covered with gold, that once belonged to a powerful convent in a town founded in 1531 by Spanish conquistador Córdoba. Mexico is an incredible mix of Mayan ruins and temples, colonial churches, missions, cathedrals, and convents.

# Culture and the Arts

In this colorful and exotic part of the world, it seems as if the exciting art forms of Spain and Portugal have been refired in the Latin American heat, lending them a potency unequaled anywhere else. Every celebration and festival bears witness to this as dazzling costumes, music, and dance positively explode onto the streets.

Dance, in particular, has its own special flavor as dancers move to vibrant lively rhythms. Indeed, the very term Latin American is often first associated with these flamboyant dances—like the samba, tango, Brazil's bossa nova, or the paso doble so popular in Colombia, having been inspired by bullfighting marches first played in southern Spain.

*Above: The La Boca neighborhood near the old port of Buenos Aires in Argentina was first settled by Italian immigrants who worked in the warehouses and meat-packing plants here. Now it has become a much-favored haunt of artists, with its pressed-tin and timber houses and lamps painted in stunning rainbow colors.*

*Left: Bumba Meu Boi, a popular festival in Brazil since the late 18th century, began in the sugar plantations and cattle ranches from whence it spread. It celebrates a story of the death and resurrection of an ox through music and dance (in particular, samba competitions) with parades and the prominent use of the colors blue and red.*

## Music, Art, and Crafts

With the interweaving of so many different cultures, Latin American music evolved into an amazing blend of styles, incorporating early Spanish Baroque as well as African drumbeat rhythms. Hispano-Caribbean music includes salsa and reggae with the lilting melody of Caribbean steel bands and calypso. Each Latin American nation has its own genre, with the haunting pan pipes of the Andes being an especially evocative sound as music curls out from ten or more pipes of gradually increasing length.

The distinctive sound of Latin American guitars (as well as similar instruments called cuatros and bandolinas) has inspired many classical guitar festivals and encouraged some superb virtuoso playing. Maracas originated in South America—they were first made from dried gourd shells filled with beans or beads.

Initially, the art of painting after the time of colonization was greatly influenced by Italian masters, Spanish, Portuguese, and French Baroque painting, and, much later, the Russian Constructivist Movement influenced Latin America's 20th century masters. Today, Latin American art is exciting and original. Many galleries and museums offer the opportunity to explore an artistic tradition that includes the fascinating works of Mexican painter Frida Kahlo (1907–1954) who so vividly depicted both her own life and the Mexican culture in which she grew up, and those of her husband Diego Rivera.

Art in pre-Columbian America included amazingly detailed carvings and patterns that have been found at Mayan, Aztec, and Peruvian sites while brilliant masks, Tepehuano yarn paintings, lacquerware, textiles, and folk art are still fabricated in all the Latin American nations. Peru's textiles, traditional tapestries, and intricate weaving designs are brilliant reminders of the Inca heritage. The flourishing tourism industry provides a ready market for colorful artifacts, such as jewelry, clay bowls, and dishes from turn-of-the-century Guatemala, wooden Voodoo carvings, Mexican pots, or papier mâché skeletons. Papel picado, a Mexican art of paper-cutting, creates lattice-like designs from tissue paper, often to celebrate religious festivals and national holidays.

**Opposite:** *Tango performances can be seen in the streets. This powerful rhythmic dance originated in Buenos Aires (Argentina) and Montevideo (Uruguay), and from there it spread to the rest of the world.*

**Below:** *Bowls for sale in a Mexican market blaze with many brilliant hues and decorative details. Textiles woven here can be just as colorful.*

# Celebrations and Festivals

In Brazil, on New Year's Eve, thousands attend a religious festival on the beaches, especially in São Paulo, Rio de Janeiro, and Bahia, to honor the goddess of the sea. Tables encircled by candles are laden with gifts and are later carried into the sea as offerings. Those swept out to sea bode well; if they return to shore, it is a bad omen.

The festival of the Virgin of Candelaria is celebrated in Chile, Venezuela, Uruguay—and in Peru and Bolivia where the Virgin is also known as the Dark Virgin of the Lake. A particularly big event is held at Puno in Peru on the shores of Lake Titicaca and at Copacabana village in Bolivia with parades, music, and a good deal of drinking. New vehicles are brought in from all over Bolivia to be blessed and anointed with beer at Copacabana!

Most famous of all is the Fat Tuesday (Mardi Gras) carnival that ushers in the season of Lent—a noisy, energetic extravaganza with street parades, elaborate costumes, music, dance, and exhibitions. Rio de Janeiro's event (see also page 192) is the most famous. Here, with the samba beat ever dominant, is a special Samba Parade. Many Brazilians spend the entire year preparing floats, costumes, and dances for their Greatest Show on Earth, a dazzling spectacle with drums, singing, and an explosion of colorful costumes. Schools and businesses close so everyone can enjoy the wild celebrations.

Barranquilla in Colombia hosts South America's second largest carnival with a grand parade, masks, folk dancing, songs, and salsa music resounding through the streets where thousands gather to join the party. Venezuela celebrates in similar style with music, balloons, and lavishly costumed parades.

The devil dance in Oruro, Bolivia, honors the patron saint of miners but it originated in Andean ancestral invocations to Pachamama (Mother Earth), Tio Supay (Satan Uncle), and the Candelaria Virgin. Here, for some ten days in a former silver-mining Andean city, music plays and there is a ceremonial parade that lasts for 20 hours without a break. Over 400,000 people come to watch 20,000 dancers and 10,000 musicians perform in this vibrant spectacle.

*Above left: Huge feathers create a stunning effect on both the headdress and costume of this performer at Brazil's Bumba Meu Boi festival.*

*Left: This samba dancer at a Brazilian carnival wears a wildly colorful headdress in vibrant pinks and oranges and a glittering costume.*

*Opposite: A girl in a feathered costume enjoys the Barranquilla carnival in Colombia—a riot of street dances and masquerade parades.*

*Above, right, and opposite:* Rio de Janeiro's riotous and world-famous five-day carnival marks the beginning of Lent as the city indulges in an explosion of revelry, after months of preparation. Some 300,000 foreign visitors pour in to watch Sambadromo events, thousands of spectacular floats and parading samba dancers flowing by in a continuous stream. There are hundreds of drummers, singers, dancers, and live music everywhere. Food and drink stalls, barbecues, and bars supply an endless source of refreshments while events include carnival balls, open-air dances, and competitions, plus orchestra and band performances. Wild costumes and pulsating Latin American rhythms let everyone know that, night and day, this is Rio party time!

## Day of the Dead

In Mexico in particular (but also Brazil, Guatemala, and Bolivia) on the Day of the Dead family and friends remember deceased friends and relatives. Folk art, skeletons, skulls, and devils decorate home altars and cemeteries. There are masks and artifacts made of sugar, clay, and wood, as well as offerings to the dead in the form of books, rattles, banners, and crosses—while the favorite foods and beverages of the departed are also enjoyed. These celebrations date back thousands of years and can trace their origins to an Aztec festival dedicated to the goddess Mictecacihuatl (the Lady of the Dead). In Bolivia, the skull of a family member may be kept at home to watch over the family and protect them all year. On November 9 it is crowned with fresh flowers and offered thank-you tokens, cigarettes, and alcohol.

A common symbol of the Day of the Dead celebrations is the skull which people represent in masks and models, called calacas (a colloquial term for 'skeleton'), and in food treats such as sugar or chocolate skulls, which often have the name of the recipient inscribed on the forehead. Sugar skulls are gifts that can be given to both the living and the dead.

*Opposite:* The Day of the Dead celebrations embody a mixture of Christian and pre-Hispanic traditions. Offerings are dedicated to the deceased and huge parades fill the streets of Mexico City.

*Below:* Tracing their origins from Aztec imagery, calacas skulls are frequently displayed with marigold flowers and foliage. As with other aspects of the Day of the Dead festival, calacas are generally considered to be joyous rather than mournful figures.

# Archaeological Sites

Latin America is blessed with a wealth of wonderfully evocative ancient remains to explore, many found in dramatic settings such as Machu Picchu perched high in the Andes mountains and Mexico's Mayan city of Tulum set above turquoise seas. These breathtaking archaeological sites have revealed many pre-Columbian treasures and feature spectacular Mayan, Aztec, and Inca temples, palaces, and strongholds.

Following on from important Peruvian cultures like the Chavín, Paracas, Nazca, Moche, and Wari—the fabled cities of the Incas in Peru were home to amazing hoards of glittering gold. During the 16th century, the Incan empire reached its point of maximum expansion, giving its rulers lordship over a territory that now comprises six countries.

*Above: Steep stairways ascend the four sides of the ancient pyramid temple at Chichén Itzá. At the spring and fall equinox, the rising and setting sun on the building's corner casts a serpent-shaped shadow along the side of the northern staircase that seems to slither down the pyramid as the sun moves across the sky.*

*Left: Early evening sunlight gilds the amazing ruins at Machu Picchu, some 7710ft (2350m) above sea level on an Andean mountaintop. Agricultural terraces and aqueducts follow the natural slopes while religious buildings rise impressively on the summit.*

# Peru's Treasure

To serve this immensely rich society, many buildings were constructed and thousands of archaeological sites dot the country, including 10,000-year-old 'camp sites' once occupied by early hunters. Caral, a 5000-year-old site north of Lima, is one of the oldest known urban centers in the Americas. 10th-century pyramids, platforms, and numerous mounds abound within the vast city complex at Túcume while the ancient stone fortress of Kuelap, built by the Chachapoyas or Warriors of the Clouds, encompasses over 400 stone buildings with zigzag decoration, all hidden behind a vast protective wall and set deep in the Peruvian jungle.

Some 11,150ft (3400m) above sea level is Cuzco, South America's archaeological capital and its oldest continuously inhabited city. It is full of steep crooked streets and monumental stone walls that date from the 16th-century Inca city. The Spaniards preserved the basic structure (developed by the Inca ruler, Pachacutec, into a complex urban center) but raised Baroque churches and palaces over the Inca stonework. The Inca work is among the best in the world, needing no mortar as the carefully shaped stones fit so tightly together. Ultimately the Spaniards made Lima the seat of the Spanish viceroyalty (until the country obtained its independence from Spain in 1821) and the legacy of colonial Peru is found in the many churches and mansions they built in both of these amazing cities.

Ancient Machu Picchu, set mountain-top high and almost in the clouds, receives 2500 visitors daily and is the most visited archaeological site in South America. It was rediscovered in 1911 by American archaeologist Hiram Bingham who was led there by a local resident. This renowned Inca site was a sacred place long before it was chosen by the Incas to be a secret ceremonial city and astronomical observatory. Agricultural terraces, watered by natural springs, flow down from the cloud-shrouded ruins of palaces, baths, temples, stores, and some 150 houses, made of mountain granite. Many of the carved and sculpted building blocks weigh over 50 tons each.

*Above right: Tambomachay near Cuzco, sometimes called the Bath of the Incas, was a sacred site dedicated to their water deity. The superb ancient Incan architecture still remains with canals, aqueducts, waterfalls that flow through terraced rocks, and spring-fed fountains.*

*Right: Once the heart of the Inca Empire, the Sacred Valley near Pisaq village has fascinating ruins. Incan mythology tells how their founder, Manco Capac, established the Inca Empire in this area. Partridges, after which both village and ruins were named, gather here at dusk.*

***Above:*** *A rainbow arches above Cuzco ruins during a reenactment of Inti Raymi, an important Inca festival celebrating the Sun god and the fertility of the earth.*

***Left:*** *Hatunrumiyoc wall, Cuzco, has a famous 12-angled stone that fits perfectly within the surrounding palace masonry.*

## Moche, Chimú, and Nazca

Gold-rich tombs can be visited at amazing Sipán in Northern Peru, rich with Moche jewelry, masks, and scepters, now housed in its extraordinary museum shaped like a Moche pyramid north of Chiclayo. Here the objects of a royal Moche tomb that somehow escaped five centuries of looting were discovered by Walter Alva in 1987. They include the tombs of the king and priest (figures depicted on ceramics and murals throughout the empire) plus gilded metal banners and hundreds of gold, silver, copper, textile, and feather objects buried alongside the Lord of Sipán.

Set in the Moche Valley, about 300 miles (480km) north of Lima beside the Andes foothills, is Chan Chan, erstwhile capital and nucleus of 12th-century Chimú culture and probably the largest mud-built city in the world—now a UNESCO World Heritage site. Here are scattered city and palace remains, cemeteries, wide streets, and walled compounds.

The famous Peruvian site of Chavín de Huántaz gave its name to the culture that flourished between 900 and 200 BC in a high Andes valley. The site contains complex terraces and squares, with dressed stone buildings. Just as complex and even more mysterious are the strange lines and huge geoglyphs which are found in the Nazca desert and Pampas de Juman in Peru. Believed to have been created between 200 BC and AD 600, they depict on an enormous scale stylized spiders, monkeys, fish, sharks, llamas, lizards, and hummingbirds as well as geometric shapes. The largest figures measure nearly 886ft (270m) in length. They are virtually unrecognizable at ground level and can only really be appreciated from the air (hence their occasional attribution as the work of extraterrestrial visitors). They may have been used for rituals, possibly related to astronomy, but their purpose remains an enigma.

Another possible early astronomical site, only recently discovered, is found at Amapa, Brazil, where 127 evenly-spaced blocks of stone, each weighing several tons, were driven into the ground on a hilltop, rather like a crown 30m (100ft) in diameter. It may have been a place of worship or an observatory and the configuration does seem to suggest sophisticated astronomical knowledge.

*Below:* The Chan Chan ruins near Trujillo, Peru, probably constitute the world's largest pre-Columbian adobe (mud) city. This was the Chimú empire's center with wonderful palaces and wide streets where some 30,000–50,000 people once lived.

## Marvels of Chile and Bolivia

Chile's Atacama Desert contains the ancient remains of an indigenous human culture in the form of carved figures of humans and animals etched on barren hillsides. Los Quilmes in Argentina is an impressive fortified city, located on a natural formation carefully chosen by its builders, the Quilmes tribe. In Patagonia, Argentina, hidden away in Cueva de las Manos (Cave of the Hands), is some amazing cave art, perhaps created 13,000 years ago, with stenciled outlines of human hands as well as vivid depictions of animals and hunting scenes.

Bolivia's Samaipata hill southwest of Santa Cruz has many carvings and was probably the ceremonial center of the 14th–16th century town here, dominated by a huge sculptured rock. Bolivia also boasts monumental remains at Tiwanaku city near the southern shore of Lake Titicaca, a capital that from AD 500 to 900 dominated a large area of the southern Andes.

*Right: Peru's Nazca lines trace amazing lines and geometric patterns across the high desert plateau. Many are on a vast scale; humans, monkeys, spiders, and many other creatures have been depicted by the careful removal of the reddish surface pebbles to reveal pale earth beneath.*

*Above: Sipán in Peru has glorious Moche tombs, rich with silver, gold, and jewelry. Here a warrior-priest's remains are draped with a necklace that features webs—the spiders have human faces on their backs.*

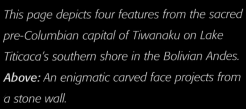

This page depicts four features from the sacred pre-Columbian capital of Tiwanaku on Lake Titicaca's southern shore in the Bolivian Andes. **Above:** An enigmatic carved face projects from a stone wall.

**Left:** The powerful structure of the entrance to Kalasasaya, the Temple of Stopped Stones, a building with amazing acoustics.

**Top:** This monolithic gateway—the Sun Gate or Calendar Gate—was built by an amazingly advanced culture in this most ancient place, now a UNESCO World Heritage Site.

**Above:** This white stone face has witnessed a succession of cultures and might once have observed the worship of the supreme Inca god Viracocha—the 'creator of civilization.'

## Amazing Mexican Sites

Countless archaeological sites in Mexico include places once inhabited by Maya, Aztec, Toltec, Olmec, and other ancient cultures. The ruined Mayan city of Chichén Itzá is located on the Yucatán Peninsula. Its main pyramid is aligned so that shadows and sunlight form the shape of a serpent's body slithering down the stairways from the peak to the earth at each equinox. This was a center of Mayan pilgrimage for over 1000 years and, in its time of greatest grandeur (AD 800 to 1200), served the Yucatán (and probably all of southeastern Mesoamerica) as the center of political, religious, and military power. The Mayan pyramids here are over 1500 years old. The Great Pyramid of Cholula near Puebla city in central Mexico, is the largest pyramid in the world and is even older than those at Chichén Itzá. Construction began in the 2nd century BC on the temple dedicated to Quetzalcóatl and carried on until the 16th century.

*Above and below:* The pyramid at Uxmal, and detail of carved stonework. Much of this pre-Columbian city, founded about AD 500, was built with well-cut stone and was an important location into the mid-15th century.

Mayapán is another Yucatán Mayan site and it served as a political capital from around 1220 to 1450, when it was sacked, burned, and abandoned. Some 11,000 to 15,000 people lived within the walled city, which contained around 3500 residential buildings and covered an area of 1.5sq miles (4km²). Also in this region, the cities of Kabah (which peaked in AD 800–900) and Uxmal are connected by a ceremonial causeway. The ruins feature elaborate carvings of the rain-god Chac. Uxmal was constructed by the Maya in the 10th century and features the Pyramid of the Magician and the Nunnery Quadrangle. There is much beautiful and intricate geometric stonework and decorative carvings to be found at this impressive site.

The grand ceremonial city of Monte Albán in southern Mexico was raised on a flattened mountaintop overlooking Oaxaca Valley, while Palenque is a Mayan site in the state of Chiapas with superb examples of Mayan architecture situated in a dramatic natural setting. In AD 683, King Pakal was entombed in a magnificent burial chamber here but the crypt under the Temple of the Inscriptions lay undiscovered until 1952.

*Above:* Temple of the Sun, Palenque—an ancient Mayan site with graceful buildings set on a ledge high above a swampy plain.

*Opposite above:* The entrance to the spectator galleries at Chichén Itzá's Great Ballcourt, the largest Mayan example in Mesoamerica.

*Opposite:* Mayan ruins at Chichén Itzá. The city experienced two main periods of occupation—from AD 495 to 692 when the architecture was truly Mayan and from 948 to 1204 when the Toltec influence emerged.

# Cities of Splendor

The remains of Templo Mayor (the Great Temple) were discovered and excavated in 1978 in the heart of Mexico City, and thousands of fascinating Aztec artifacts have been found here. Constructed by the Aztecs in the 14th century, it was the major religious site for nearby Teotihuacán—an important and vast Aztec city. The Aztecs believed the gods created the universe here and so built the magnificent temple complex (from about 100 BC). Here stand the vast and imposing Pyramid of the Sun, the Pyramid of the Moon, and the Avenue of the Dead.

Beautifully located on a clifftop overlooking the Caribbean, Tulum is another superb Mayan site. Protected by walls to deter invasion, it flourished between AD 1200 and 1450. Visitors now can appreciate temples, a city square, and wonderful murals.

In the depths of Colombia's Sierra Nevada jungle lie the ruins of a lost city. La Ciudad Perdida was only rediscovered in the 1970s by treasure hunters who followed a series of stone steps up a mountainside. Possibly founded around AD 800, it rose on terraces cut into the steep mountains and access entailed climbing up 1000 steps and crawling through carved tunnels to reach the city. It has narrow tiled roads and circular town 'squares.' Its population may have numbered some 8000 people at its peak and many gold statues and items of jewelry have been found here.

**Above:** The lost city of Ciudad Perdida in Colombia dates back to the 9th century AD. It may once have been home to around 10,000 people.

**Opposite:** Tulum was a Mayan fort and city. It was protected by steep sea cliffs as well as its enclosing 26ft (8m) thick walls.

**Below:** The Pyramid of the Sun at Teotihuacán, a huge edifice in a vast pre-Aztec city which features a truly magnificent temple complex.

## Awe-inspiring Giants

Easter Island, which lies 2237 miles (3600km) west of Chile, is famous for its hundreds of giant human figures, carved from rock and known as moai. These mysterious enigmatic statues, which date from about AD 1000, have angular eyeless faces but archaeologists have recently discovered that coral eyes with dark stone pupils originally filled the empty eye sockets. The largest statue is 32ft (9.9m) tall while one unfinished figure found in a quarry would have risen 68ft (21m) high. It seems that these massive figures were venerated as objects of worship by the islanders.

There are stone figures in Colombia too, in San Agustín, where expertly carved human forms and depictions of jaguars, snakes, frogs, great birds, and monsters assume variously serene, wise, or frightening characteristics as they smile, frown, or sneer. This important pre-Columbian ceremonial center is considered by archaeologists to be one of the most significant ancient sites in Latin America. Human figures can also be seen in the National Archaeological Park of Tierradentro in Colombia, which contains many huge 6th to 10th-century burial chambers and underground tombs, decorated with motifs and geometric patterns.

*Left and above:* Monumental statues, called moai, stare out to sea from Easter Island's Rapa Nui National Park, a World Heritage Site since 1995.

# Latin American Cities

In an area as vast as Latin America, there are many vibrant and exciting cities to attract the visitor, each with its own distinct character. Unfortunately, there are far too many to include them all here so these following portraits can serve only as an enticing starter, leading the reader from (roughly) north to south on a journey of discovery.

## Havana

Cuba's capital is Havana which is the largest city in the Caribbean. It was founded in 1515 by Spanish conquistador Diego Velázquez de Cuéllar. It soon became a principal port for trade in emeralds, mahogany, and spices. As a convenient harbor for treasure-filled galleons setting sail from the New World, the ships and the city became frequent targets for attack by pirates. Today it is a grand old place, sometimes dusty and crumbling in the sunshine but oozing character and history.

***Above:*** *Lively Copacabana beach is set in the heart of Rio de Janeiro, Brazil, and is backed by busy streets, hotels, and restaurants with some featuring grand Art Deco architecture among the modern buildings.*

***Left:*** *Havana, Cuba's capital, boasts gloriously faded paintwork on grand buildings with arcades, columns, balconies, and magnificent vistas in what was—in the days of piracy—the most heavily fortified city in the Americas.*

## Old Havana and Trinidad

Old Havana (now designated a UNESCO World Heritage Site) boasts elegant colonial architecture and wonderful arcades, a vibrant Chinatown, glorious classic American cars dating from the era before Fidel Castro came to power in 1959, a wedding-cake-ornate cathedral, cigar factories, and many atmospheric bars serving rum cocktails as they did in days gone by to famous author Ernest Hemingway.

Also in Cuba is the UNESCO World Heritage site of the city of Trinidad, founded in 1514. Horse-drawn carriages tour lovely cobbled streets edged by pastel-colored houses ornamented with elaborate wrought-iron grilles. It is one of the best-preserved Caribbean cities, enriched by the sugar trade and distinguished by many elegant palaces and plazas. For a time it was Cuba's wealthiest city.

## Santo Domingo

Set at the mouth of the Ozama River in the Dominican Republic this is the Americas' oldest continuously inhabited European settlement and the first seat of Spanish colonial rule in the New World. It was founded in 1496. Despite attacks by Francis Drake and subsequently by pirates, it has survived five centuries of turbulent history and was the departure point for countless voyages of discovery. It has cobblestone streets, ancient walls, a Spanish palace, a cathedral (the first Catholic cathedral in the Americas) and fortress, wonderful botanical gardens, and, supposedly, the remains of Christopher Columbus in an impressive tomb housed in a lighthouse. Their provenance is disputed, however; others claim that his remains were moved to Seville in Spain. Santo Domingo was, in fact, founded by Christopher Columbus' brother, Bartholomew.

**Above:** *Trinidad in Cuba oozes charm and past glories with its elegant colonial squares including the Plaza Mayor, cobbled courtyards, historic buildings, ornate balconies, red terracotta-tiled roofs, shady porches, bars, restaurants, and bands playing traditional music.*

**Opposite:** *A turquoise painted façade with wrought-iron balconies and window railings in intricate twists and swirls. The old blue automobile is a reminder that Havana, one of Latin America's best-preserved colonial cities, is renowned for classic American cars.*

## Mexico City and Acapulco

Mexico City is the world's third largest and most populated city with over 20 million people living in its greater metropolitan area. The city was built on the dry bed of Lake Texcoco, surrounded on three sides by high mountains and volcanoes, including the tongue-twister Mount Popocatépetl. Earthquakes are a common phenomenon here. The city dates back to 1325, when the Aztec capital city of Tenochtitlán was founded. It was destroyed in 1521 by Spanish conqueror Hernán Cortés but rebuilt to serve as the New Spain Viceroyalty capital for three centuries. Today it is famous for its many superb palaces and stately buildings and has the largest number of museums and the largest park (Chapultepec) within any city, as well as floating gardens that have been here for seven centuries—since the time of the Aztecs. About 30 miles (50km) to the northeast are the ruins of Teotihuacán—some of the world's biggest ancient pyramids have been found in this Aztec City of the Gods.

Acapulco is one of the world's most exciting beach cities and ports, located on a deep, semicircle of a bay on the southwestern coast of Mexico. The site has been inhabited since before 3000 BC but was discovered by Spanish expeditionary leader Francisco Chico in 1521. It was claimed for Spain by Hernán Cortés in 1531. Often attacked by pirates seeking the treasure traded during its annual merchants' fair—as well as by Sir Francis Drake in 1579 when he unsuccessfully attempted to capture Spanish galleons there—Acapulco became a major trading center for cargos of spices, ivory, silks, and porcelain. It was the main depot for the Spanish fleets voyaging out to trade with Asia.

**Above:** *Acapulco, once a Spanish fleet depot, is now a vibrant beach resort, known for its daring divers who plunge from the cliffs into the sea.*

**Opposite:** *Granada's fine squares and plazas are flanked by Spanish colonial buildings.*

## Managua, León, and Granada

The capital of Nicaragua is Managua but León and Granada steal the historical prizes as two of the oldest cities in Latin America, both founded in 1524 by Francisco Hernández de Córdoba—and rivals for national supremacy ever since. León, threatened by the erupting Momotombo volcano and a severe earthquake, moved west to its present site in 1610. Despite looting by pirates in 1685, it flourished. Its ancient landmarks include a tamarind tree, more than 600 years old now and once used as gallows. Granada is set by Lake Nicaragua, the second largest Latin America freshwater lake. This is the oldest mainland city established by the Spanish conquistadores and is renowned for its lovely colorful houses and impressive colonial-era architecture.

## Panama City

Founded in 1519 by Pedro Arias Dávila, Panama City became a convenient center for the Spanish exploration and conquest of Peru and then a useful port for the despatch of gold and silver to Spain. It attracted pirates, including the notorious Henry Morgan and his 1400 men who looted and destroyed the city in 1671. A new city was built slightly to the west of the old site. The spread of new railroads in the 19th century and the construction of the Panama Canal in 1904–14 increased its prosperity and today it is a bustling international banking center. Its public transport system consists of brightly painted buses, often customized to depict famous performers or politicians. Panama's canal is justifiably famous, and the splendid ruins of Old Panama are a popular tourist destination where remnants of the first Spanish settlement on the Pacific Ocean still remain.

## Caracas

Venezuela's capital sits in a bowl of green forested hills. In many ways it is a chaotic place, encompassing the extremes of wealth and poverty and it has the unfortunate reputation as being one of the most dangerous cities in Latin America. There are soaring skyscrapers in the busy city center while shantytowns sprawl over the surrounding hills. Francisco Fajardo, the son of a Spanish seafarer, first tried to establish a plantation here in 1562 but was expelled by the locals. Five years later, Spanish captain Diego de Losada founded Santiago de León de Caracas, with cocoa cultivation becoming its main activity. The famous champion of South American independence Simón Bolívar was born here in 1783.

*Below:* High-rise buildings spike the skyline in modern Panama City near a glorious coastline of palm-fringed beaches and tropical forests.

## Quito

Set high in the Andes, perched on the slopes of the volcano Pichincha (and regularly threatened by this), Quito is Ecuador's capital and the world's second highest capital after Bolivia's La Paz. It lies at an elevation of 9350ft (2850m). It was a thriving town as long ago as the first millennium when it was occupied by the Quito tribe and was conquered in succession by the Caras tribe, the Incas, and ultimately, after great resistance, the Spanish under Francisco Pizarro. It gained independence in 1822 after the battle of Pichincha when troops under Simón Bolívar's leadership defeated the Spanish forces. Like its volcano, Quito has remained a volatile place, subject to unrest and where scenes of poverty are seldom far from view.

*Below:* Quito, Ecuador's capital city, sprawls chaotically some 9350ft (2850m) high across the slopes of an active stratovolcano.

*Above:* Orange and ocher hues blaze in shanty-town houses seemingly piled one upon another on a steep hillside in Caracas, Venezuela.

## Lima, Cuzco, and Iquitos

Here are three very different Peruvian cities. Lima is the nation's capital, founded in 1535 by Francisco Pizarro. It served as the conquistadores' vital headquarters—its coastal location helping to maintain easy communication with Spain—and then grew into the commercial and administrative center of the Spanish empire. Following devastation in an earthquake in 1746 (only 20 houses survived), it was rebuilt with wide streets, huge plazas, and elegant homes with ornate balconies. In the 20th century roadbuilding allowed a huge wave of migrants to move to the city and its population now stands at more than 8 million.

Cuzco (see also page 168), erstwhile center of the Sun cult and capital of the Inca Empire, is today a UNESCO World Heritage Site, once described by Francisco Pizarro as a 'very noble and great city,' and as having, '… such fine buildings that it would even be remarkable in Spain.' Nearby are many amazing ruins at Machu Picchu, the Sacred Valley, and steep terraced hillsides that are a reserve for thousands of native Peruvian plants, including potatoes that were first cultivated in Peru during Incan times.

Iquitos is the largest city in the Peruvian rainforest, a hot humid place surrounded by three rivers and the first Amazon river port—its claim to fame being that it is probably the most populous city in the world to be accessible only by river. It developed from a 1750s Jesuit mission and then blossomed because of its thriving rubber industry. Gustave Eiffel (of Eiffel Tower fame) built the House of Iron in the Main Square here. This house made of prefabricated metal sheets had been originally constructed for the Paris Exhibition in 1889 and was subsequently shipped in pieces to Iquitos by a wealthy tycoon. Iquitos remains the tourist center of eastern Peru. Nearby are Amazon rainforest nature reserves and at the edge of the city is Belen, called the Peruvian Venice because of its floating houses built on rafts and others perched on stilts that extend down to the river bed.

**Opposite:** *At night the dramatic façade of Lima's Basilica Cathedral glows by the main plaza. In 1535 conquistador Francisco Pizarro carried the first log on his shoulders and placed the first stone to launch this great construction.*

**Left:** *In the wet season Belen (in Iquitos) is accessible only by boat. Buildings are on stilts or float on rafts, tethered to large poles as they rise with the water. Some homes float year-round on the Amazon waters.*

**Below:** *Mountains tower around the red roofs of Cuzco, the Inca capital from the 13th century. The city has, some say, the outline of a puma. The conquering Spaniards preserved the original structures but built Baroque churches and palaces on top of the Inca ruins.*

## Sucre and La Paz

The judicial capital of Bolivia is in Sucre (formerly La Plata) which boasts a wealth of colonial architecture. It is renowned for fossils of dinosaur footprints found in a quarry here, so much so that a statue of a dinosaur now greets tourists at the airport. La Paz is Bolivia's administrative capital and also boasts many wonderful museums, palaces, churches, a cathedral, and an excellent market. Founded by conquistador Captain Alonso de Mendoza in 1548, La Paz rose on the site of an ancient Aymara village. In this 'city that touches the clouds' the buildings scramble up the mountains and are set at an altitude of 10,650–13,250ft (3250–4100m) which makes it the globe's highest capital city.

*Above: A colonial-style balcony in La Paz, Bolivia. In 1898, La Paz was made the seat of the national government, with Sucre remaining the nominal historical, as well as judicial, capital.*

*Right: A glittering night panorama of La Paz, Bolivia, a vibrant fast-expanding city set high in the Cordillera Real de los Andes mountains and so nicknamed 'the city that touches the clouds'.*

## Brasília, Rio de Janeiro, and São Paulo

Brazil has several amazing cities, with Brasília being the present capital and one of the newest hubs in a continent of many ancient cities. It was inaugurated in April 1960, after centuries of careful planning, and is set on a plateau in the middle of the country with wonderful architectural masterpieces that, when seen as a group from the air, assume the shape of an aeroplane or butterfly.

The River of January, Rio de Janeiro, was the capital of Brazil from 1763 to 1960, serving both the Portuguese colony and then the independent nation as the country's principal city. An accidental landfall by Pedro Álvares Cabral, en route to India, led to the establishment of this Portuguese Brazilian colony. Today Rio is famous for its spectacular natural setting, with the outstretched arms of the giant statue of Christ the Redeemer on the peak of Corcovado mountain seeming to embrace the magic of the city below. It was recently named one of the new Seven Wonders of the World. Rio is also renowned for its beaches (including Copacabana and Ipanema), Sugarloaf Mountain with its famous cable car, the vast Maracanã football stadium (one of the world's biggest), and its two forests—Tijuca is the largest city-surrounded urban forest and the globe's second largest urban forest, while the world's greatest urban forest is in the Parque Estadual da Pedra Branca. Even more famous are the New Year celebrations and fireworks here, as well as Rio's amazing riotous carnival held on Mardi Gras, launched first by a masked ball in 1840 (see also page 161).

The first Jesuit missionaries arrived in São Paulo in 1554, founding a village and mission. Later coffee plantations and the export of their produce would enrich this city until today it is South America's biggest by population and the world's seventh largest, with a skyline dotted with many impressive skyscrapers. A lively cosmopolitan place, here they perform Brazil's dance-like martial art, *capoeira*. It is also a thriving center for libraries, theaters, and publishing houses. Its 20 million inhabitants encompass many races; it is said to be the greatest 'Japanese', 'Portuguese', and 'Spanish' city outside Japan, Portugal, and Spain and the globe's third largest 'Italian' and 'Lebanese' city outside Italy and Lebanon!

**Opposite:** *Rio de Janeiro's Morro da Urca (Urca Hill) tramway station offers a magnificent view of the Sugarloaf peak and its cable car. Verdant tropical forest scrambles below with azure sea and purple islands beyond.*

**Left:** *Brasília's cathedral was designed by Oscar Niemeyer, the 'sculptor of monuments' involved in planning the city and many of the buildings in this UNESCO World Heritage Site.*

**Below:** *Lights twinkle all around the curve of Botafogo Bay and its white beach, sheltered from the Atlantic Ocean by the Urca peninsula and Sugarloaf mountain.*

## Buenos Aires

This seductive city port on the Río de la Plata (River Plate) was discovered in 1516 and founded as a city in 1536, following an expedition there led by Spaniard Pedro de Mendoza. Today this is the gateway to and capital of Argentina, with bustling cobbled streets, grand avenues, elegant buildings, a magnificent opera house, and many cafes and stylish restaurants in which to enjoy the famous Argentinian steak. The amazing and colorful pressed-tin and wooden houses in La Boca are painted in stunning rainbow hues—these days the region is famous for its artistic community. There are treasure-filled antique shops while the strains of tango emanate from bars redolent with cigar smoke.

*Opposite: The famous Obelisk is situated in the Plaza de la República—a vast city square in the heart of Buenos Aires—on the Avenida 9 de Julio. This impressive avenue is named in honor of Argentina's Independence Day (July 9, 1816) and is one of the widest in the world, measuring some 460ft (140m) across.*

## Asunción

The capital of Paraguay—popularly known as the Mother of Cities—is one of Latin America's oldest cities and the longest continually inhabited one. Set along the Paraguay River in the River Plate basin, it was from here that colonial expeditions departed to found many other cities. It takes its name from the Feast of Assumption (Asunción), which was the day when the first stockade was established. Today antique cranes are still busy in the harbor while jacaranda and flame trees gleam in the riverside park. Multicolumned palaces and official buildings line the Bay of Asunción while the city is graced by fine plazas, magnificent mansions, and late 19th-century Belle-Époque buildings with delicately decorated façades and balconies. The amazing Mercado Quatro market sells everything from wedding dresses, computers and software to sweet potatoes.

*Below: La Boca (Buenos Aires) is a Mecca for artists, tourists, and photographers with its multicolored wood, tin, and zinc houses.*

## Santiago

Chile's capital was founded in 1541 by Spanish conquistador Pedro de Valdivia. The Mapuche destroyed it just six months later but soon the Spanish returned to rebuild the city. Today it has a dramatic skyline of high-rise office towers, particularly in its thriving financial area, set against a backdrop of glinting snowy Andean peaks. There are stunningly modern underground trains and highway systems and, despite enduring many battles and earthquakes, beautifully maintained colonial buildings. The city is conveniently close to Pacific beaches, ski centers, and the world-famous Maipo Valley vineyards.

## Montevideo

The capital of Uruguay, an area once hotly disputed by Spanish and Portuguese invaders, ultimately became a Spanish slave port. Set on the north shore of the River Plate estuary, Montevideo developed into a charming cosmopolitan city encompassing Spanish, Italian, and Art Deco styles plus many vestiges of colonial times in its Ciudad Vieja (Old City). It has beautiful beaches, a fine harbor (site of the scuttling of German warship, the *Admiral Graf von Spee* in 1939) and is a great place to see tango dancing. The port here handles most of Uruguay's export trade.

*Above:* The bustling harbor at Montevideo, capital of Uruguay. The city is a pleasing mix of colonial Spanish, Italian, and Art Deco styles.

*Right:* Santiago in Chile is a busy city with a fine transport system. Night traffic streams past glass towers and mountain peaks catch the moonlight.

# Cultivation and Commerce

Such is the diversity of the landscape in this immense conglomeration of nations that the traditional way of life, away from the cities, assumes a great many forms. Its variety reflects both geography and different national characteristics. Many people live a rural life, some in isolated villages, or in farmsteads perched on hillsides or amid pampas lands—or perhaps on desert fringes, or working in seaside and fishing communities. Some have settled on islands, alongside rivers, or deep in the jungle. Others live in the high Andes and have adapted, over generations, to surviving in the thin air found at altitude. Indigenous Indians from Peru and Bolivia have developed increased lung power and capacity so that their hemoglobin-richer blood can transport higher levels of oxygen—for them, altitude sickness is not a problem.

*Above:* The capsicum (chile pepper) plant is indigenous to South America, where they grow wild. The Spaniards found that drying and crushing the pods of the hottest chile peppers made an excellent fiery substitute for the peppercorns that were extensively used in European cooking.

*Left:* The blue agave is a succulent plant that is an important economic product of Jalisco state in Mexico. It is the base ingredient for the alcoholic drink tequila. The heart of the plant is removed, stripped of leaves, heated, and pressed to remove the sap, which is then fermented and distilled.

**Background:** *Palm trees in Punta Cana, in the Dominican Republic, fringe miles of beautiful white sand beaches on a coastline freshened by gentle breezes.*

**Below:** *Captain Bligh of HMS Bounty fame first brought breadfruit to the Caribbean to serve as an inexpensive food source for slaves.*

**Opposite left:** *Traditional Mexican pottery and textiles are sold at local markets.*

**Opposite right:** *Historic Paraty (or Parati) in Brazil is a World Heritage Site set beside tropical forests, mountains, and an emerald green sea dotted with tropical islands.*

# Towns, Villages, and Countryside

There are delightful villages in the Dominican Republic and other Caribbean islands, such as Cuba that has fertile valleys and distinctive limestone hills that rise out of the landscape as softly rounded as pin-cushions. Village life in the Caribbean often involves growing coconuts or fishing. A great variety of fruits flourish here—pineapple, papaya, passion fruit, and football-sized breadfruit that were first introduced by Captain Bligh (of 'Mutiny on the *Bounty*' fame) to the Virgin Islands.

In southern Mexico, many ethnic groups have retained their traditions and folklore, some practicing ancestor worship, sorcery, or traditional medicine. Others recount legends of demons and animal spirits that live in rivers, forests, mountains, and sacred caves that have long formed part of their oral history. Mexican craftspeople make all sorts of wood and clay items, as well as toys, reed flutes, hammocks, nets, baskets, polished and decorated gourds, clay dolls, and seed necklaces. Their dances may symbolize fights between bulls and jaguars or tell the story of the Malinche woman who served Hernán Cortés during the Conquest as both his interpreter and mistress. Local economy is based on cultivating coffee, corn, beans, squash, potatoes, vegetables, pears, or tomatoes, or raising pigs and poultry.

Along the Amazon river and in the depths of the rainforest lie remote villages where being able to hunt successfully is a vital skill; an in-depth, intuitive knowledge of wildlife may be the key to survival. Far from hospitals and medical aid, it is fundamental to know which plants are edible or make good medicines and those which are highly poisonous; how to move through the jungle silently and find a safe way home again; which snakes, spiders, and frogs are deadly and which of the noxious ones—like poison-arrow frogs—offer useful toxins to apply to arrow tips.

Brazil's coast is home to a totally different kind of village life. At the UNESCO World Heritage Site of Paraty (once a colonial export center for gold and diamonds mined inland) there are no cars, only donkey-drawn carts trotting along narrow cobblestone streets, some of which were deliberately engineered so that they would flood with incoming seawater on the day of the full moon.

About 600 miles (1000km) off the coast are lovely islands including the rugged and untouched Trindade with its deserted beaches and waterfalls where tribal village life continues as a delightful mix of old traditions with just a few concessions to 21st-century ways.

# Rural Life

Throughout Latin America, farmers and fishermen gather to sell their produce in local markets, sometimes arriving heavily laden after they have traveled considerable distances with their goods over difficult terrain or through thick forests. These markets offer an opportunity for handworkers to sell craftwork, silver or, as in Peru, ponchos, hats, stuffed llama dolls, pan pipe flutes, and other souvenirs. Useful foods, tools, and baskets will also change hands.

Many valleys in Peru fairly bustle with vibrant villages and festive market days as farmers, craftsfolk, coffee growers, tribal women, and families gather to set out their wares for sale— woolen weavings, alpaca textiles made on traditional looms, bright belts, silver filigree, and carved gourds *(mates burilados)* etched with scenes of Andean life are all on offer. Relaxing afterward, a traditional Andean menu may offer delicious soup with beef, egg and noodles, broiled alpaca meat, or tea made with coca leaves.

In the fertile pampas lands of Argentina, where tired gauchos once rested in the shade of the straggling ombu bushes, stretch vast fields of cultivated alfalfa, sorghum, wheat, maize, corn, soy, or sunflowers under endless bright blue skies and scudding clouds. Here on the huge prairies are raised thousands of head of cattle. This practice led to the creation of dairy farms and historical estancia ranches displaying fine colonial architecture and large estates. Set on both sides of the River Plate, they offer visitors a magnificent setting for discovering life on the pampas.

In northwestern Argentina, the uplifted Sierras Pampeanas extend over the central region, with mountain ranges enfolding valleys, streams, and stretches of fertile agricultural land. Meanwhile, in Argentina's Calchaquíes Valley, quiet villages snuggle into green valleys dotted with simple adobe and thatch houses, an unchanging scene despite the passing centuries. Beyond lies a contrasting arid landscape, with amazing wind-sculpted rock formations in semidesert surroundings.

Chile, too, has beautiful isolated mountain valleys and colonial villages made recently wealthier by the boom in wine production and export of agricultural produce. Traditional festivals here include rodeo and colt-taming events. There are plentiful apple, cherry, peach, and plum orchards—and wonderful vineyards, especially in the Maipo Valley where ancient villages cling to mountainsides above a river that courses from the Andes to the Pacific. The Casablanca Valley climate is ideal for growing grapes, as is the Great Aconcagua Valley where avocados, peaches, plums, and kiwis flourish while the mountains are mined for gold, silver, and copper, as they have been since Incan times.

*Above:* Peruvians have carved gourds (called mate) for some 3500 years.

*Opposite:* A woman working at a loom in Peru wears richly colored traditional dress trimmed with buttons and decorative braid.

*Right:* Glorious Mexican hats are for sale in a local craft market.

**Left:** *A Chilean vineyard. The finest pisco (a regional brandy) is made from grapes grown in the Elqui valley—an area which enjoys around 300 days of sunshine every year.*

**Above:** *Wine storage barrels in Chile where the wine industry is much respected and expanding rapidly. Chile's wine regions include eight separate valleys, each with its own characteristics, where grapes are grown that flourish in the long dry summers.*

## Sugar, Tobacco, Coffee, and Cocoa

Sugar cane is one of the oldest cultivated crops in the world, said to have originated some 3000 years ago in New Guinea. Today it is grown in many Latin American countries with huge crops being found in places like Guatemala. The climate on Peru's northern coast is ideal for producing sugar cane and it has also long flourished in the Caribbean—ever since it was introduced by Christopher Columbus and observed to thrive in the climate here. Sugar was very much entwined with the slave trade, its production relying on slave labor in places like Hispaniola (now Haiti and the Dominican Republic) where the first record of sugar cane being grown in the New World was recorded in 1505.

Tobacco is widely cultivated in Honduras, Nicaragua, Ecuador, Mexico, Brazil, and the Caribbean—including Puerto Rico and the Dominican Republic where it is mainly grown in the Cibao river valley. It thrives in several parts of Cuba but especially in the rich red soil of Vuelta Abajo—acclaimed as the world's best black tobacco region. Here both climate and soil are ideal for the harvesting of this aromatic plant, its unique aroma being the hallmark of the fine cigars with which Cuba is famously associated.

Coffee is grown in Costa Rica, Cuba, Ecuador, Mexico, Peru, and Venezuela, but Brazil is famous for being the world's largest coffee producer, responsible for over 40 percent of global supplies. Its best crops are grown in the São Paulo region. Colombia is the world's third largest producer of coffee (after Brazil and Vietnam), supplying vast quantities of high-quality beans and producing more Arabica coffee than any other nation. As the cultivation of coffee in Brazil grew, so did slavery—as an ever-increasing demand for coffee prompted the Brazilian government to import thousands of slaves. By 1828 well over a million of them, nearly a third of the population, worked on coffee plantations.

Cotton has been grown in Latin America for centuries. Its seeds are able to float on the sea and remain viable for several years so plants may have originally spread to the continent by this method. Certainly, it was growing in Latin America by the late 15th century. The Aztecs gave their baby daughters spinning tools at birth and most could spin proficiently by the

*Below: Tall sugar canes growing in Brazil, today the major sugarcane-producing nation. Sugar canes were first brought to the Caribbean by Columbus during his second voyage of discovery.*

time they were four. Peruvian cotton is of the highest quality, often produced for export, while Argentina is now South America's largest cotton producer, with Brazil close behind.

Cocoa, which is made from the seeds of the cacao tree—a native of dense tropical forests—originated in the Amazon basin and then spread from Brazil and Mexico (cultivated by the Mayas and Aztecs) and into other parts of Central America and the Caribbean. It has played a significant economic and social role for some 2500 years and today it is grown in Brazil, Colombia, the Dominican Republic, Ecuador, Mexico, and Venezuela. Some 500,000 families in Latin America depend on the crop for their livelihood.

*Above:* Tobacco plants thrive in the rich red soils of Cuba. In the past, tobacco served the local people as a type of miraculous medicine and was also used in religious, political, and social ceremonies.

*Right:* The people of Latin America have been smoking cigars since the 10th century. Spanish conquistadores took tobacco back to Europe and the manufacture of cigars has long been a renowned Cuban specialty.

## The Fruits of Land, Sea, and Forest

There is a great outpouring of produce from Latin America with countless fruits and vegetables, dairy items, meat and livestock being exported to markets around the world. Raising beef for export is a vital part of the economy for Argentina, Uruguay, Paraguay, and Colombia, while Uruguay also exports wool and hides, as does Argentina—along with corn and linseed.

There is prime fishing off the Pacific coast, where the sea is a major source of anchovies and tuna, while other Latin American Atlantic and Pacific hauls include pejerrey (a kind of mackerel), golden dorado, immense yellow-and-black-spotted catfish, squid, and hake. Waters off Ecuador are rich in tuna, marlin, and many other fish that thrive where the cold Humboldt current (having swept up the South American coast, carrying a rich store of nutrients, plankton, and krill) meets the warmer currents around Central America. Ecuador exports large quantities of tuna and shrimp, and Guayaquil Bay's warm waters host many commercial shrimp farms.

Timber has always been a hugely important natural resource in South America. Today, growing fears are expressed over mass logging causing the depletion of Amazonia's green mantle and its impact upon worldwide climate change, which puts many wildlife species at risk. Sustainable forest management is becoming increasingly crucial. Well-structured forest plantations should bring economic development and reduce pressure on native forests, while providing much-needed timber products as well as vital employment. A variety of such programs to introduce responsible forestry have been instigated in many Latin American countries.

*Opposite above: Fishermen haul in their nets on the Patagonian coast.*

*Opposite below: Chiles drying on the roof of a house in Guatemala.*

*Below: Forestry and logging has long been a major industry in Brazil but today must be controlled to prevent widespread Amazon deforestation.*

## Natural Resources

Spearheaded by Brazil, several Latin American countries are developing their biofuel industries, hoping to reduce global warming by offering alternatives to fossil fuels. Companies in Costa Rica and El Salvador import sugarcane-based ethanol from Brazil, processing and then shipping the fuel to the US. Guatemala will soon have five sugarcane-based ethanol plants while Argentina plans to convert soybean oil crops into biodiesel exports. Colombia produces an annual 95 million gallons (360 million liters) of ethanol and aims to create fuel from palm oil, too, while Chile is researching the feasibility of turning wood chips into ethanol. As Cuba modernizes its ethanol refineries, Peru plans to produce 36 million gallons (136 million liters) a year by 2010. Many US and Caribbean vehicles already run on ethanol/gasoline blends.

Mineral resources in South America are plentiful and include gold, silver, copper, iron ore, tin, and oil, while diamonds are mined in Brazil, Guyana, and Venezuela. The Atacama Desert in Chile boasts some of the world's largest open copper mines at Antofagasta and Chuquicamata. In the past Chuquicamata's rich copper and mineral deposits produced a huge natural supply of sodium nitrate (saltpeter) but this supply has been exhausted in some areas, so now the desert is littered with abandoned mining towns.

## Tourism in Latin America

Tourism, too, is a vast and growing industry. While the Caribbean has long been a popular vacation destination, today many other Latin American areas are opening up to tourism, making previously inaccessible places viable and exciting vacation destinations. The tourist industry is booming, as many visitors discover the fascinating history and wildlife here or enjoy the pristine beaches, natural wonders and vibrant cities. More active tourists may enjoy vacations where they can ride horses on the pampas or join a charter boat trip to fish for marlin and sailfish in the ocean.

Many tourists come simply to relax at popular resorts like the Mexican Yucatán Peninsula coast or Copacabana in Brazil. There are now dozens of high-end resorts and deluxe hotels, including vast luxurious vacation complexes near Cancún in Mexico, while Cuba attracts thousands to its white sand beaches. 'Ecotourism' is also developing—its proponents aim to welcome visitors who want to experience nature at first hand while protecting the fragile balance of the natural habitat in such special places as the Amazon basin.

*Background:* A beach at Cancun, Mexico, on the Yucatán peninsula—a tropical paradise enjoyed by some four million visitors each year. Divers and swimmers especially appreciate its crystal-blue Caribbean seas.

**Above:** Huge trucks carry ore from the contours of an open-pit copper mine at Calama in northern Chile's Atacama Desert. The ore is extracted from the levels in the mine by using controlled explosions.

**Above:** An exclusive resort in Mexico offers superb beaches as well as visits to Mayan sites and the jungle. Cancún alone has about 140 hotels and 380 restaurants but visitors are advised to avoid the hurricane season.

# Final Thoughts

This virtual visit to Latin America began with a sweep along the coastline, discovering sparkling white beaches, delicate coral reefs, palm trees tossed by soothing breezes, and islands set like jewels in a sapphire sea. Beyond these shorelines luxuriant forests rise, sometimes dense Amazon jungles aglow with brilliant parrots, hummingbirds, and the gleam of an elusive golden jaguar. We have glided along silver rivers, been deafened by tumultous waterfalls, gazed at awe-inspiring mountain peaks and erupting volcanoes, discovered vast pampas lands, swamps, deserts, and glistening salt flats.

Latin America has such a wealth of splendid natural wonders plus a rich tapestry of historical incident and cultural heritage woven into its fabric. This tour has revealed incredible archaeological sites—pyramids, temples, and palaces in ancient cities where Mayans, Aztecs, Incas, and countless other civilizations once flourished. We have explored exciting cities, seen dazzling carnivals and flamboyant dances. Following in the wake of pioneering adventurers and explorers, we have discovered the magic of one of the most exciting regions in the world.

*Above: The outline of Alpamayo peak rises in the Cordillera Blanca mountains, a steep pyramid of ice and snow that shimmers in sunlight.*

*Right: In the Bolivian Andes, morning light tints the world's greatest salt flat where a giant prehistoric lake stretched some 40,000 years ago.*

# Fascinating Facts

Figures do vary, depending on the sources, and some are subject to change as conditions alter with time, but the following facts provide some interesting sidelights on Latin America:

## Geography and Landscape

• The Amazon is the second longest river in the world (after the Nile), stretching 4000 miles (6435km) and accounting for up to 20 percent of the total volume of freshwater flowing into the world's oceans each year.

• The Amazon region boasts the largest area of tropical rainforest in the world. Here the jungle covers about 2,300,000sq miles (600 million hectares). However, some estimates predict that if the destruction of the forest is not halted, it may all have disappeared by within 40–50 years.

• Brazil's forests constitute some 60 percent of the Amazon forest, which also stretches into Bolivia, Columbia, Ecuador, Peru, and Venezuela.

• Costa Rica has a 802-mile (1290km) coastline with 132 miles (212km) of Caribbean coast and 670 miles (1078km) on the Pacific.

• The seemingly endless Pacific coastline of Chile stretches over 4000 miles (6435km) north to south.

• The Atlantic Ocean makes a massive 4650-mile (7490km) sweep around Brazil.

• Mexico's coastline is world famous for big waves that attract brave surfers, hoping to ride rollers that can measure up to 40ft (12m).

*Above:* A surfer rides a giant wave that crashes onto the Mexican coast.

*Opposite:* Latin America includes those territories in the Americas where the Spanish or Portuguese languages prevail: Mexico, most of Central and South America, plus Cuba, the Dominican Republic and Puerto Rico.

• The pampas region of South America is one of the world's most important grasslands, covering an area of more than 295,000sq miles (760,000km$^2$).

• The Andes mountains are second only to the Himalayas with regard to their size and height. The range stretches over 5500 miles (8900km) from the Caribbean coast of northern Colombia, running through Ecuador, Peru, Bolivia, and (in the north) Venezuela to the southern tips of Argentina and Chile. The Andes encompass active volcanoes and many peaks over 20,000ft (6100m) in height. Its zenith is Mt Aconcagua at 22,831ft (6959m) on the border of Chile and Argentina.

• The world's highest free-falling waterfall is the Angel Falls in Venezuela where the water plummets a total of 3212ft (979m), with a clear drop of 2648ft (807m).

• Costa Rica's Arenal volcano is highly active and is probably the most spectacular in Latin America with glowing red lava flowing from its crater, high ash columns, and small eruptions almost daily. It is one of the ten most active volcanoes on the globe.

• In the Bolivian Andes, the world's largest salt flat sparkles at Salar de Uyuni. It lies on the Altiplano and measures 4085sq miles (10,582km$^2$) in area and contains an estimated ten billion tons of salt.

*Above:* Ecuador—a waterfall tumbles between crags and thick forest.

# Wildlife

• Some researchers believe that 30 percent of the animal biomass of the Amazon basin is made up of ants.

• Of the world's nearly 1000 species of bats, only three species are vampire bats but all of these live in Latin America.

• An armadillo digging underground can hold its breath for up to six minutes.

• Possibly one in five of all the birds in the world live in the Amazon rainforests. Around 2000 species of mammals and birds have been scientifically classified in the region, as well as more than 40,000 plant species and some 2.5 million insect species.

• Brazil is home to the globe's biggest known spider, the Goliath bird-eating spider *(Theraphosa leblondi)* that can have a leg span of up to 11in (28cm).

• Latin America is also home to the globe's smallest spider; a fully adult male *Patu digua* from Colombia measures only 0.015in (0.37mm) in length.

• Galápagos giant tortoises can live for over a century and may weigh up to 550lb (250kg).

*Above: Contorted rock formations in Ischigualasto, Argentina.*

• Adult green iguanas can reach up to 6.5ft (2m) in length and are called tree chickens as a result of their being served as a food by native populations for some 7000 years.

• The jaguar is the western hemisphere's largest and most powerful big cat. An adult male may grow to 6ft (1.8m) in length, not including its 30in (75cm) tail.

• Owl monkeys *(Aotus* species) are the only nocturnal New World monkeys: their large eyes provide them with excellent night vision.

• Spectacled bears live in forested mountains and have occasionally been found at altitudes of up to 13,800ft (4200m). Their diet includes mice, rabbits, birds, berries, grasses, orchid bulbs, and the leaves and hearts of bromeliad plants. They will even climb cacti in the search for food, clambering up over the sharp spines to reach the fruit at the top.

• Scarlet ibis *(Eudocimus ruber)* live in tropical South America and the Caribbean. As their name suggests, both male and female adults have brilliant bright-red plumage. It is the national bird of Trinidad.

• Ischigualasto in northwestern Argentina has many amazing natural rock formations and has revealed some of the most exciting and most ancient dinosaur fossil bones ever found dating from the Late Triassic over 200 million years ago.

*Left: A superb blue and gold macaw surveys the Amazon rainforest—the Earth's largest and home to one in ten of our planet's recorded species.*

## Plants

- The Amazon jungle has between 50 to 200 different tree species per 2.5 acres (1 hectare) with an estimated total of 2500 tree species being found there.
- Many familiar garden plants, shrubs, and flowers originated in Latin America, with orchids being among the most prized specimens, but also bougainvillea, passionflower, begonia semperflorens, and pampas grass. Berberis and buddleia originated in the Andes.
- An estimated 438,000 species of plants of economic and social interest have been registered in the Amazon with many more remaining to be discovered or cataloged.
- Potatoes, rubber, tomatoes, tobacco, and chocolate first came to Europe from Latin America.
- In the Amazon's shallow river waters and lakes, the giant water lily *Victoria amazonica* grows. Named for Queen Victoria, its leaves can measure up to 10ft (3m) in diameter on 22–26ft (7–8m) long stalks.

## People, History, and Architecture

- The term Latin America was first used by French Emperor Napoleon III (Charles Louis Napoléon Bonaparte) in the 1860s but was not commonly used until the early 1900s.
- Today Brazil has a population of around 185 million people. Some five million indigenous people are believed to have lived in Brazil in the 16th century. Today, there are around 350,000 Indians in Brazil representing more than 200 tribes.
- Simón Bolívar was a famous general and liberator who organized and led military forces to free the northern portion of South America from Spanish rule in the early 19th century and after whom Bolivia is named.
- Football is a national obsession in Brazil; the country has won the World Cup five times.
- UNESCO World Heritage Sites in Latin America include 29 in Mexico, 17 in Brazil, 10 in Peru, and 8 in Argentina.
- Mexico's Chichén Itzá Pyramid has been named as one of the new Seven Wonders of the World, along with Rio de Janeiro's Christ The Redeemer statue and Peru's Inca fortress city of Machu Picchu. These sites were selected in an online campaign organized by the New7Wonders Foundation which attracted more than 100 million votes.
- The Pyramid of the Moon in the ancient city of Teotihuacán in Mexico actually consists of seven pyramids, built one atop another. Below lies a burial chamber with the remains of 12 people (ten are decapitated) five wolf or coyote skeletons, three puma or jaguar skeletons, and 13 bird skeletons.
- When the Panama Canal opened in 1914, it reduced the Atlantic/Pacific sea route by some 7000 miles (11,200km).
- The Incas built an incredible road and rope bridge system looping over the Andes. Runners, called chasquis, carried messages along these roads in a series of human relays allowing communications to be sent over long distances very quickly.
- In 1532 the Spanish conquistador Francisco Pizarro defeated the Inca ruler Atahualpa (regarded as a direct descendant of the Sun) and his army of some 80,000 warriors. Despite overwhelming odds, Pizarro seized the vast Inca empire with an army of less than 200 men and the complicity of some local collaborators.
- In Tikal, Guatemala, there are towering Mayan pyramids. The Temple of the Great Jaguar, Temple I, rises nearly 212ft (65m) high, while the largest structure at Tikal, Temple IV, is approximately 230ft (70m) tall.

*Left:* Latin America is home to over 20,000 orchid species—the example shown grows in the Ecuadorian Andes. The complex biology of orchids makes them excellent indicators of the overall biodiversity in an area.

# Latin American Timeline

For reasons of space and simplicity, when the term 'discovers' is used here, it implies European (not Amero-Indian) discovery.

### Earliest times

30,000–20,000 BC: Hunters and gatherers cross the Bering Strait land bridge and enter North American continent.

10,000 BC: Further migration across the Bering Strait. Now groups spread south across the American mainland to Chile.

8000–2000 BC: Large Ice Age game, such as mammoths, disappear. Agriculture and village life begins to be established.

4500–3500 BC: Maize and cotton are being cultivated in Mexico.

3500–1700 BC: Early ceramics and fertility figurines made in Ecuador.

2000–400 BC: Olmec culture in Mexico produce hieroglyphic writing and monolithic stone heads.

800–200 BC: Chavín in Peruvian highlands create art, ceramics, and weavings.

### Classic period

200 BC–AD 1000: First cities appear.

AD 200–600: Paracas culture on south Peru coast; mummified bodies wrapped in finely woven textiles. Nazca lines created near the southern Peruvian coast. Moche civilization on north Peru coast decorates pottery with realistic painting.

AD 300–900: Maya civilization flourishes in Mesoamerica—skills include astrology, calendrics, maths, and writing. Monte Albán, Mexico—city built on vast high platform is one of Mesoamerica's earliest and will be a vital Zapotec center for some 1000 years.

AD 450–750: Teotihuacán, Mexico—Pyramids of the Sun and Moon built in this vast city.

AD 600–800: Huari, Peruvian Highlands—rise of large cities and empires.

AD 600–1000: Monolithic stone architecture erected at the city of Tiwanaku, Lake Titicaca (Bolivia).

### Post-classic period

950–1150: Empires grow; many wars. Toltecs dominate central Mexico.

1000–1476: Chimú empire, Peru—city at Chan Chan represents Latin America's largest prehispanic mud-brick settlement.

1200–1225: Inca emperor Manco Capac and his sister Mama Ocllo found Cuzco—Inca Empire established.

1225–1532: Inca empire develops highly sophisticated administration.

1325: City of Tenochtitlán founded by Aztecs.

1345–1521: Aztecs create tribute empire in Mexico.

1415–60: Prince Henry the Navigator launches Portuguese Age of Exploration.

1425–c.1438: Incas establish cult of creator god Viracocha.

1438–1471: Incan emperor, Pachacuti, expands empire south from Cuzco valley, transforming a small state into a formidable nation.

1440–1487: Emperor Montezuma I expands Aztec empire.

1471–1493: Inca ruler Tupac Yupanqui defeats Chimú (1476) and extends empire to coast and south to Chile.

1487: Dedication of Great Temple in Tenochtitlán, Mexico.

### Conquest and colonial periods

1492: Christopher Columbus lands in Hispaniola and discovers the Americas. After he leaves, his remaining forces pillage and rape in Hispaniola. Native Americans retaliate and Spaniards all killed. 400 years of fighting will ensue.

1493: Columbus' second voyage—explores Hispaniola, Cuba, and Jamaica.

1493–1527: Inca emperor Huayna Capac expands empire north to Ecuador and Colombia but his death from smallpox leads to civil war between sons Huascar and Atahualpa.

1494: Treaty of Tordesillas established by Pope Alexander VI divides New World between Spain and Portugal.

1496: Spanish found Santo Domingo, Hispaniola, the first Spanish town in the Americas.

1498: Colombus explores coast of Venezuela.

1499–1500: Amerigo Vespucci voyages to South America.

**Above:** *Patagonia's Cueva de las Manos has stencilled images of human hands dating from 550 BC, as well as 9000-year-old hunting scenes.*

1500: Pedro Alvares Cabral claims Brazil for Portugal: military campaigns at northern and southern edges of Inca empire.

1502: Montezuma II becomes emperor of Tenochtitlán.

1503: Jews escape Portuguese Inquisition by emigrating to Brazil.

1507: German cartographer Martin Waldseemüller publishes New World map, using the name America to honor Amerigo Vespucci.

1508–09: Puerto Rico subjugated by Spanish explorer Ponce de León.

1510: Vasco Núñez de Balboa founds Santa Maria la Antigua del Darien, the first permanent European settlement on the American mainland.

1511: Spanish seize Cuba despite indigenous resistance.

1513: Vasco Núñez de Balboa's expedition across Panama isthmus. He is the first European to see the Pacific Ocean from New World.

1516: Juan Díaz de Solís is the first European to explore the Río de la Plata (River Plate).

1517: Francisco Hernández de Córdoba leads Spanish expedition to Yucatán in Mexico.

1519–22: Hernán Cortés lands in Mexico and conquers the Aztec capital Tenochtitlán.

1520: Mexico—Montezuma II collaborates with Spanish but is either killed by them or pelted with rocks by his own people (accounts differ). Ferdinand Magellan sails Straits of Magellan and is the first European to see Tierra del Fuego.

1521: Tenochtitlán, Mexico, succumbs to Spanish and their Indian allies.

1522: Spanish Gil González Dávila explores Nicaragua. First slave revolt in Hispaniola.

1524: Council of the Indies established by the Spanish king Charles V to administer colonies.

1525 Inca civil war caused by struggle for succession to throne.

1532: Peru—Atahualpa wins civil war and proclaims himself Inca emperor.

1532–33: With just 180 men, Francisco Pizarro captures Atahualpa, ending Inca Empire and seizes Inca capital, Cuzco.

1533: Spaniards found Cartagena (Colombia).

1534: Rumiñahui leads Inca resistance against Spanish.

1535–50: Antonio de Mendoza is first Viceroy of New Spain.

1536: Gonzalo Jiménez de Quesada explores Nueva Granada (Colombia).

1536: Diego de Almagro explores Chile.

1536–37: Inca uprising in Peru defeated by Almagro (he will be defeated in battle in 1538 by rival conquistador Francisco Pizarro and executed).

1537: Spaniards found Asuncíon (Paraguay).

1538: Spain establishes New Granada colony (Colombia).

1538: Jiménez de Quesada founds Santa Fe de Bogota (Colombia).

1541: Spanish conquistador Pedro de Valdivia founds Santiago in Chile.

1541: Francisco de Orellana sails through the Amazon river system from Ecuador to the Atlantic and names a tribe of female fighters Amazons, thus giving a name to the region and river.

1542: Spanish Crown issues New Laws to protect Indians.

1542: Francisco de Montejo the Young conquers most of Yucatán for Spain.

1544: Civil wars in Peru.

1545: Spanish crush Maya revolt.

1550–53: Spanish colonists from Peru led by Francisco de Aguirre found Santiago del Estero, Argentina's first permanent European settlement and oldest city in the country.

1552: Cattle, imported into Paraguay, spread to Argentina.

1555: Spanish settlement in Havana, Cuba, attacked by French. French colonists build fort in Rio de Janeiro bay—Portuguese will expel them in 1565.

1562: War with Indian population in Brazil.

1567: Spaniards found Caracas in Venezuela.

1570–71: Inquisition established in Lima and Mexico City.

1571–72: Peru—revolt of Tupac Amaru I. Last Inca rebel stronghold, Vilcabamba, captured by Spanish.

1572: Francis Drake attacks Spanish ships and harbors in the Caribbean.

1573: Juan de Garay founds Santa Fé (in present-day Argentina).

1574: There are now 160,000 Spaniards in America.

1576: Smallpox epidemic in Mexico kills over 1 million.

1577: British seafarer Francis Drake raids Valparaiso (Chile) and in 1580 completes second circumnavigation of world.

1580: Juan de Garay refounds Buenos Aires which had been abandoned in 1541. First Jesuit missions among Guaraní in Paraguay.

1586 Sir Francis Drake attacks Santo Domingo in Hispaniola and Cartagena in Colombia.

1616: Dutch explorer Willem Schouten establishes route around Cape Horn connecting the Atlantic to South America's western coast on the Pacific.

1617: Paraguay separated from Argentina.

1627: Dutch capture Spanish silver fleet en route from New Spain.

1668: British pirate Henry Morgan raids Panama. In 1670s Morgan and his buccaneers capture Spanish treasure awaiting shipment at Puerto Bello, Panama.

1693: Gold rush after gold is discovered in Brazil.

1697: Spain cedes western part of Hispaniola to France.

1700: Philip V becomes king of Spain—new Bourbon dynasty demands greater powers in colonies and more revenue derived from them.

1713: Utrecht Treaty permits Britain the exclusive right to export African slaves to the Spanish colonies (1200 a year to Buenos Aires) for 30 years.

1717: Spain establishes vice-royalty of Nueva Granada (Colombia, Ecuador, Venezuela) with capital in Bogotá.

1722: Dutch Admiral Jacob Roggeveen discovers Easter Island.

1742–55: Peru—revolt of Juan Santos Atahualpa, self-proclaimed descendant of Inca who organizes resistance to Franciscans and colonial authorities.

1750: Treaty of Madrid recognizes Brazil's borders and shifts Spanish-Portuguese dividing line to allow Portugal further expansion to the west.

1759: Jesuits expelled from Brazil.

1767: Expulsion of Jesuits from the Spanish empire.

1776: Spain creates new vice-royalty of the Río de la Plata (Argentina, Uruguay, Paraguay, and Bolivia) with capital in Buenos Aires.

1780–81: Revolts in Upper Peru and Colombia—repressive measures in their wake destroy wealth and status of traditional Indian nobility.

1791: Haiti slave revolt devastates sugar industry so exports boom in Brazil as a result.

1795: Spain forced to cede Santo Domingo (half of Hispaniola) to France.

1799–1803: German geographer and naturalist Alexander von Humboldt explores Mexico and South America.

1806–07: British troops seize Buenos Aires from Spain but are expelled.

1809–25: Unrest in Bolivia.

1810: Simón Bolívar leads independence movements in South America. Creoles establish ruling juntas in Caracas, Venezuela, Santiago, Chile, and Buenos Aires, Argentina.

1810: Mexico—War of Independence against Spain begins.

1811: Venezuela and Paraguay declare independence from Spain. Unrest in Uruguay.

1813: Mexican Congress formally declares Mexican independence.

1815: Simón Bolívar forced to retreat to Jamaica.

1815–20: Unrest in Colombia.

1816: Argentina declares independence. Brazil invades Uruguay.

1818: Chile declares independence.

1821: Dominican Republic (Spanish half of Hispaniola) declares its independence from Spain. Country is invaded by Haiti.

1822: King Pedro I declares Brazil independent from Portugal: Ecuador achieves independence from Spain.

1823: United States under President James Monroe issues Monroe Doctrine warning Europe not to attempt to recolonize or interfere with the newly independent Spanish American nations.

1825: Bolivia declares independence and is named to honor Simón Bolívar.

1827: Chile has five revolutions in one year.

1828: Peru invades Bolivia. Colombia declares war on Peru. Brazil is defeated by Uruguay and Argentina. Uruguay gains independence.

1829: Colombia and Bolivia win war against Peru.

1834: Civil war in Peru.

1835: Bolivia's dictator Santa Cruz conquers Peru. Brazil's War of the Farrapos starts as Republicans oppose the succession of Dom Pedro II.

1836: Texas declares its independence from Mexico and war erupts. Chile fights Peru and Bolivia.

1838: The United Provinces of Central America dissolved— Costa Rica, El Salvador, Guatemala, Honduras, and Nicaragua become independent.

1838–42: France attacks Mexico. Civil war begins in Uruguay. Chile defeats Peru and Bolivia.

1844: The Dominican Republic declares its independence from Haiti.

1845: Brazil's War of the Farrapos ends.

1845: Texas annexed by United States.

1846–48: Mexican-American War. Mexico defeated; northern half of Mexico ceded to US (New Mexico, Nevada, Arizona, Utah, and California) as part of peace treaty.

1851: A military coup installs General José María Urbina as dictator of Ecuador.

1851–52: Colombia and Uruguay abolish slavery.

1853: Peru annexes Amazon forest area claimed by Ecuador.

1855: US mercenary William Walker occupies Nicaragua; he rules for two years but is ultimately shot by Honduran firing squad in 1860.

1855: United States builds Panama railway linking Atlantic and Pacific coasts.

1858–61: Mexican Civil War—the War of the Reform.

1859: Unrest and civil war in Argentina and Mexico. Peru occupies southern Ecuador.

1861–65: Over 13,000 Hispanics fight in the American Civil War.

1862: British, French, and Spanish troops attack Mexico; Britain and Spain withdraw but War of the French Intervention begins.

1862–63: Ecuador and Colombia at war; Ecuador defeated.

1863: British ships blockade Rio in trade war to force Brazil to free slaves. France defeats Mexico.

1864–70: War of the Triple Alliance—Argentina, Brazil, and Uruguay attack Paraguay.

1864: France crowns Archduke Maximilian of Austria emperor of Mexico but he is overthrown and executed in 1867 when Liberal armies defeat Empire forces and reestablish a republic.

1870: Paraguay surrenders to Argentina, Brazil, and Uruguay after over half of its population (300,000 people, most of the male citizens) had been killed in war.

1876: Porfirio Díaz seizes Mexican presidency; his dictatorship lasts (with one four-year period of interruption) until 1911.

1879: Civil war in Colombia—80,000 people die.

1879–84: War of the Pacific as Chile fights Peru and Bolivia over mineral resources. Ultimately, Bolivia loses access to the sea and saltpeter fields to Chile; Peru is bankrupted and loses its southern provinces to Chile.

1888: Brazil is the last nation in the western hemisphere to abolish slavery.

1889: Brazil proclaimed a republic after coup deposes Dom Pedro II.

1894: US send troops to Nicaragua. Colombia plunges into anarchy when President Rafael Núñez dies.

1895: War for Cuban Independence starts.

1896: War of Canudos in Brazil between state forces and settlers in Canudos. Civil war in Uruguay.

1898: Spanish-American War. Cuba gains independence from Spain. United States ends Spanish rule in America and takes control of Puerto Rico, Guam, and the Philippines.

1899: Civil war in Colombia.

## Modern times

1900: The US oil tycoon Edward Doheny strikes oil in Mexico.

1901: Platt Amendment gives US right to intervene in Cuban politics. Cuba also agrees to lease naval base at Guantanamo Bay to the US.

1902: Cuba becomes a republic.

1903: Panama separated from Colombia and is established as a republic.

1904–14: Panama Canal built.

1905: United States begins to administer political institutions in the Dominican Republic.

1906: Collapse of coffee prices causes economic crisis in Brazil.

1909: US Marines intervene in Nicaragua to promote US interests. Marine presence lasts until 1933.

1910: Mexican Revolution begins with uprising against Porfirio Díaz. Protracted civil war ensues.

1912: United States occupies Nicaragua.

1912–16: Contestado War in Brazil.

1917: Brazil becomes only Latin American nation to fight in WWI, supporting Britain and France. Oil discovered in Venezuela.

1924–25: United States withdraws from Dominican Republic and Nicaragua.

1926: Mexican government seizes all Catholic Church properties.

1927: Uprising in Nicaragua.

1929: Guerrilla war in Nicaragua against US.

1930: Revolutions, coups, and military takeovers in Brazil, Peru, and Bolivia.

1932: Over 1000 executed during Peru insurrection.

1932–35: Chaco War—Bolivia and Paraguay dispute border. Paraguay will annex most of Bolivia's Gran Chaco region.

1938: Mexico's oil industry nationalized, including US and British oil companies.

1941: Peru wins war about territory against Ecuador.

1945: Under Juan Perón, Argentina becomes a haven for Nazis as World War II ends.

1946–52: Eva Perón (Evita)—wife of President Juan Perón—serves as First Lady of Argentina until her death from cancer.

1956–59: Cuban Revolution. Fidel Castro installs communist regime in Cuba after years of guerrilla warfare.

1960: New city of Brasília becomes Brazil's national capital. Huge earthquake (magnitude 9.5) recorded off coast of Chile.

1961: Eisenhower administration in the United States severs diplomatic relations with Fidel Castro in Cuba. Failed Bay of Pigs invasion of Cuba by Cuban exiles sponsored by the US.

1962: Cuban Missile Crisis as United States and Soviet Union almost come to war over the siting of Soviet missiles in Cuba.

1965: United States forces occupy Dominican Republic.

1967: Cuban revolutionary Che Guevara killed by Bolivian forces supported by the CIA in Bolivia.

1968: Police and army fire on students in Mexico City—300 students killed.

1971: Mexico student riots—hundreds killed.

1972: Large reserves of oil discovered in Ecuador.

1973: General Augusto Pinochet seizes power in Chile coup that overthrows socialist government of Salvador Allende—over 3000 people will be killed or 'vanish' during his 17-year rule.

1979: Nicaragua revolution—Sandinistas overthrow Somoza regime.

1980: Guerrilla warfare in Peru.

1982: War between Britain and Argentina caused by the Argentinian invasion of the Falkland Islands.

1986: Indigenous groups in Ecuador form pan-Indian organization, CONAIE (Confederation of Indigenous Nationalities of Ecuador).

1989: United States invades Panama to depose dictator Manuel Noriega. 3000+ killed in Colombia as Medellín drug cartel oppose the Colombian government.

1994: United States, Mexico, and Canada form NAFTA (North American Free Trade Agreement). Rebellion in Mexico. Fidel Castro allows 50,000 people to leave Cuba to seek a better life elsewhere.

1998: Thousands die in Nicaragua hurricane.

2000: Honduras—over 1000 street children killed by death squads. Argentina's economy collapses.

2004: Brazil launches its first rocket into space.

2005: Brazil now the globe's fifth most populous country in the world with 188 million people—Mexico eleventh with 107 million—São Paulo and Ciudad de Mexico among world's ten largest megacities.

2006: Cuba's dictator, Fidel Castro, taken ill—his brother Raul takes charge. Chile's former military leader Augusto Pinochet dies, aged 91.

2008: Fidel Castro announces retirement. Production of biofuel in Brazil booms. Rabobank launches pilot carbon-credits scheme to encourage replanting of lost areas of the Amazon rainforest.

*Above:* São Paulo is Brazil's richest, most populous city. Its metropolitan area is Brazil's greatest—and one of the world's largest.

# Index

## Picture credits

(*l*=left, *r*=right, *a*=above, *b*=below, *c*=center, *i*=inset, *bg*=background)

© **Shutterstock.com:** 63(*r*), 82-83(*l*), 175(*br*); Abstrand 167(*r*), 174(*a*); Carlos Ameglio 45(*bl*); John A. Anderson 28(*r*); Galyna Andrushko 49(*r*), 51, 55(*al*), 212(*l*); Brett Atkins 20; AyakovlevdotCom 180-181(*l*); Thomas Barrat 189(*b*); Robert Paul van Beets 207(*a*); Simone van den Berg 77(*a*); Ben4633 29; Hagit Berkovich 6-7(*l*), 62-63(*l*), 69; Casey K. Bishop 118-119; Joel Blit 169(*bl*); Gualtiero Boffi 126-127(*l*); Vera Bogaerts 37; Sebastien Burel 21(*b*), 48-49(*l*), 55(*br*), 90-91(*l*), 121(*r*); Bryan Busovicki 1, 131(*al*); Franck Camhi 18(*al*), 18-19(*r*), 154(*i*), 156-157(*l*), 161(*a*), 177, 193(*a*); Pablo H. Caridad 11(*al*), 116(*br*); Cheryl Casey 14-15; Sam Chadwick 130-131(*l*); Wai Chan 36(*l*); Ewan Chesser 86; Schmid Christophe 16-17(*bg*); Katarzyna Citko 45(*br*); David Davis 41(*r*), 162-163(*r*); Celso Diniz 2-3; Dlrz4114 7(*r*); Jorge Luis D'Onofrio 131(*br*); Jason Scott Duggan 212-213(*r*); Erkki & Hanna 128, 184-185(*a*); Fenghui 199(*r*); Gordon Galbraith 176(*b*); Karel Gallas 216(*bl*); Alex Garaev 175(*ar*); Christos Georghiou (*graphics throughout*); Colman Lerner Gerardo 32-33(*l*), 40-41(*l*); Eric Gevaert 78-79(*r*); Andrzej Gibasiewicz 26-27; Jose Gil 165; Guentermanaus 104-105(*l*), 105(*ar*); Tomasz Gulla 144-145(*l*); Darla Hallmark 201(*il*); Jeanne Hatch 136-137(*bg*); Bill Heller (*graphics throughout*); Carly Rose Hennigan 107(*r*); Adam Hicks (*graphics throughout*); Andrew Howard 12-13; Chris Howey 10-11(*l*), 58-59(*a*), 169(*r*), 170; Imageshunter 64-65(*bg*); ImageZebra (*graphics throughout*); Kato Inowe 214(*ar*); Nathan Jaskowiak 55(*bl*); Javarman 4-5, 24-25(*bg*), 44-45(*a*), 56-57(*bg*), 114-115(*bg*), 190-191(*r*); José 171(*br*); Mariusz S. Jurgielewicz 80-81; Curtis Kautzer 131(*bl*), 138; Stephan Kerkhofs 28(*l*); Graham S. Klotz 131(*ar*); Grigory Kubatyan 173(*bl*); Kwest 196-197(*r*); Henrik Lehnerer 65(*br*); R. J. Lerich 153(*ar*), 188; Elisa Locci 58-59(*bl*); Luís Louro 61(*b*); Jason Maehl 52-53; Aleksandrs Marinicevs 25(*br*); MartinM2008 30-31(*r*); Rafael Martin-Gaitero 22-23; Jose Luis Mesa 68(*a*); Mishella 25(*al*); Dale Mitchell 157(*r*), 159(*i*); Byron W. Moore 210-211(*bg*); Christian Musat 11(*br*); Carlos Neto 73; Antonio Jorge Nunes 66-67; Oculo 164; Mark Van Overmeire 173(*br*);Damian Palus 162(*al*); Michael Pemberton 203(*l*); Mark William Penny 162(*bl*); Dan Peretz 91(*bl*); Carlos Sanchez Pereyra 198-199(*l*); Bill Perry 155(*i*); Mike Price 77(*b*); Lee Prince 74-75(*c*); Celso Pupo 154-155(*bg*), 181(*r*), 193(*b*); Dr. Morley Read 59(*br*), 72, 75(*a*), 75(*c*), 102-103; Rebvt 25(*bl*); Marco Regalia 110-111(*b*), 175(*al*); RestonImages 211(*ir*); Eduardo Rivero 11(*ar*), 21(*a*), 30(*l*), 88-89, 91(*ar*), 94, 95, 101, 106-107(*l*), 116-117(*a*), 127(*br*), 135, 209(*a*), 218; RM 83(*r*), 124-125; Elder Vieira Salles 18(*bl*); Carlos E. Santa Maria 133(*r*), 142-143(*b*), 143(*a*); R. Gino Santa Maria 76; David M. Schrader 109; Sharky 108; Joel Shawn 132-133(*l*), 141(*r*), 150-151(*l*), 152-153(*bl*), 202; Misha Shiyanov 39, 187(*b*);

Luiz Antonio da Silva 201(*br*); B. G. Smith 13(*r*); Mike Smith 64-65(*c*); Peter Sobolev 24; Jennifer Stone 158; Matty Symons 174(*b*); Charles Taylor 60, 185(*b*); Luis César Tejo 100; David Thyberg 25(*ar*), 55(*ar*), 120-121(*l*); Lee Torrens 152-153(*bl*); Matt Trommer 140-141(*l*); 153(*br*); Urosr 11(*bl*), 34-35, 114(*ia*), 159(*bg*), 160, 176(*a*), 209(*b*); VanHart 134; Ismael Montero Verdu 68(*bl*); Nicola Vernizzi 57(*il*); Joao Virissimo 200-201(*bg*); Mike Von Bergen 71(*r*); Danny Warren 57(*ir*), 166-167(*l*); Maria Weidner 161(*b*); Daniela Weinstein 46-47; Daniel Wiedemann 208; Ivonne Wierink 179(*r*); Robert Wróblewski 43; George Yu 127(*ar*); Peter Zaharov 33(*r*); Jarno Gonzalez Zarraonandia 9, 16(*ib*), 116(*bl*), 151(*r*), 168-169(*ac*), 168(*b*); Zeljana 92-93(*bg*); Dusan Zidar 182; Alexander Yu. Zotov 54-55(*l*).

© **iStockphoto.com:** Dean Bergmann 200(*i*); Bigredlynx (*graphics throughout*); Rob Broek 112-113, 211(*il*); Greg Brzezinski 91(*br*); Norberto Budnikas 136(*ib*); Franck Camhi 139(*b*); Cosmopol 216(*ar*); Craig Chiasson 139(*a*); Sonja Fagnan 196(*l*); Henri Faure 217; Fenykepez 38; Micheál O Fiachra 91(*al*); Steve Geer 84-85, 204-205(*l*); Frank Sebastian Hansen 92(*i*); Martin Harrison 122; HiM 65(*ar*); Torsten Karock 36(*r*), 78(*l*), 98-99(*b*), 99(*a*); Adrian Koeppel 207(*b*); Mark Kostich 123; Warwick Lister-Kaye 98(*a*); Luoman 221; Michael Madsen 75(*b*); Constance McGuire 145(*r*); Steven Miric 186; Alex Nikada 192, 195; Marek Pilczuk 42; Randy Plett 105(*br*); Alberto Pomares 50, 187(*a*); Morley Read (*r*), 214(*bl*); Jan Rihak 178-179(*l*), 205(*r*); Christina Rodriguez (*graphics throughout*); Sayarikuna 190(*l*); Ian Schlueter 111(*a*); Daniel F. Q. Schumaher 97(*r*); Simcoemedia 183; Alan Tobey 110(*a*); Wsfurlan 206; Michael Zysman 203(*r*).

© **Corbis:** Theo Allofs/Corbis 87, 96-97(*l*); Bettmann/Corbis 61(*a*), 146; William Coupon/Corbis 148(*l*), 148(*r*), 149; The Gallery Collection/Corbis 147; Gavin Hellier/Robert Harding World Imagery/Corbis 194; Kevin Schafer/Corbis 189(*a*); Hubert Stadler/Corbis 136(*ia*).

© **Getty Images:** Nathan Benn/National Geographic/Getty Images 171(*a*); Martin Gray/National Geographic/Getty Images 172-173(*l*), 173(*a*); Roy Toft 68(*br*).